Contents

'If you want to understand anything in Life look to the origin.'

Foreword

Why write it? Why read it?

'If you want to understand anything in Life look to the origin,' said French philosopher Rousseau.

So when wanting to understand why the subject of Brands and branding had gripped me for so many years I took his advice and looked backwards.

My mother was Italian, my father was English, I was born and bred in Brazil, and schooled in Sussex. I think I've spent all my life looking for 'home' and, as such, have always been a bit of an outsider.

The objectivity has proven to be invaluable.

The cultural, physical and climactic contrasts between Brazil and England taught me a great deal about 'differences.' And there were plenty.

To the Brazilians and the Italians I was different. To the English, especially at school, I was very different.

If Brands are about differentiation then maybe M. Rousseau was right. My own origins had offered up the first clue.

But I was sure that there was something deeper to this question than mere 'difference.'

I wanted to understand the fundamentals of something that had made me devote a working lifetime to with such passion, energy and vigour. The magnetic pull to the subject has been quasi-religious.

And therein lay another clue.

One of the more valuable lessons from my happy-go-lucky schooldays was the understanding that the world's major religions converge around the tenet 'Know Thyself.' I have long believed this is the precursor to Identity, and it's at the very core of the branding process.

On researching the origins of 'Know Thyself,' I was delighted to find that it was Socrates, no less, who pioneered it; given that first Plato and in turn Aristotle were his disciples, it came with reassuring credentials.

But it got better.

'Know Thyself' is inscribed on the Temple of Apollo in Delphi, regarded by the Ancient Greeks as the geographic centre of the world, and therefore at the centre of all human community.

ΓΝΩΘΙ ΣΑΥΤΟΝ

As such, that inscription places 'Know Thyself' at the epicentre of all things human. Not bad for importance, then.

Emboldened in my quest, a cursory look at temple-owning Apollo threw up some passable credentials too.

Son of the Supreme Greek God Zeus, he was known to be creative, handsome and a supporter of all the Arts of Civilization. Good start.

The worst that could be said of him was that he was 'all too happy to enjoy the charms of nymphs, as well as the occasional youth, and his conquests numbered in the dozens.'

Sounds like the kind of God I might enjoy a drink with.

Even Carl Jung had an opinion on the subject, with his contribution of 'he who looks outside, dreams; he who looks inside, awakens.'

So what I'd always placed at the very heart of branding was now providing me with the smug satisfaction of higher moral justification. After all, if it was a good enough handle for Apollo, Socrates, Plato, Aristotle, Jung and the world's major religions then it was probably good enough for me.

Not forgetting Rousseau's Gallic twist.

Perhaps it's not surprising that a 'Britalian' with a Brazilian tinge might feel a greater need to know himself. But nowadays, aren't we all from 'somewhere else,' whether place or upbringing?

Aren't we all searching for self-knowledge, whether individually or as organisations?

Isn't our understanding of the world fundamentally predicated by an understanding of ourselves?

And beyond self-discovery, aren't we all looking for our unique way of expressing ourselves?

It means that, like it or not, we're all actively engaged in the process of branding at one level or another.

And it explains why Brands and branding are now a global commercial phenomenon, here to stay. People want to belong, and yet they also want to stand out. Brands let them do just that.

'He who looks outside, dreams; he who looks inside, awakens.'

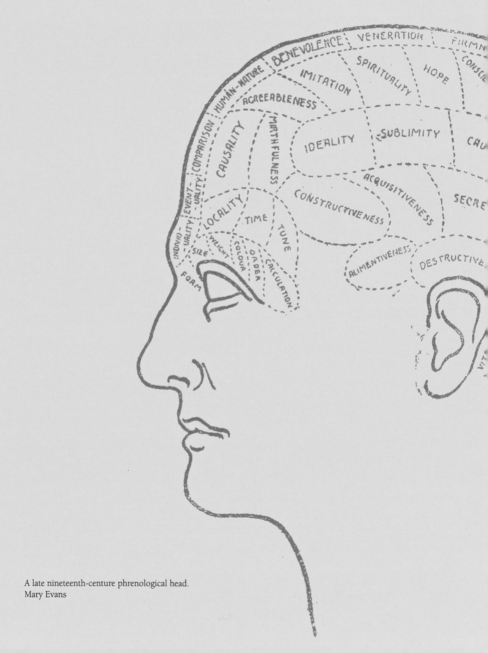

A late nineteenth-centure phrenological head.
Mary Evans

Contrary to the beliefs of some, this process is not 'spin.'

Nor is it 'the dark arts.'

Nor the flowery pursuit of dreamers or the soft-minded.

It is, in fact, nothing less than the Essence of Purpose.

And it's every bit as true for organisations as it is for individuals.

This book is a collection of stories about my own and my Clients' 'Know Thyself' trails, condensed into nine and a half golden rules. Some of the trails are bumpy, some of them smooth and many, thankfully, not yet travelled.

They're drawn from some of the world's great Brands, including BMW, BT, Honda, Unilever and The Body Shop, and they're designed to provide insights into how smart companies can use their most powerful intangible asset, their Brand, to win – on their terms.

They're also intended to share experiences that you might find familiar, useful, interesting or just enjoyable.

Hopefully you'll find something of yourself in them.

Introduction

This book is written for CEOs. Or, just as important, people who think like them.

Aside from being the only ones who can see across all the Departments, they also have the responsibility for drawing them together.

And they almost always have to do this alone. With support from others, yes, but they are where the branding buck stops, as with so many other bucks in a business.

Having the vision for the organisation, articulating it, campaigning it, persuading, cajoling, charming and, when necessary, bullying others into it, all falls to that office.

They're supposed to see the future by having their head in the clouds, and yet keep on top of day-to-day realities by having their feet planted firmly on the ground.

They need necks long enough to see round corners; and they need to be brave enough to stick them out.

And they need to get along with everyone they need to get along with, making sure that the others all get along properly with each other. But, of course, they're not allowed to get on too well with anyone.

They're like ambidextrous jugglers on a trapeze wire.

On stilts.

In a wind.

The CEO's greatest helper in this ubiquitous quest can be a well-defined and well-expressed Brand. It can and should be their reference point, their compass, their moral guide, their source of inspiration, their sword and shield in the relentless pursuit of both making their vision come alive and, ultimately, leaving a meaningful legacy.

This book is written in the spirit of offering informal advice about branding, based on real-life stories. It is not a theory-based or academic reference tome. The world doesn't need another one of those... Rather, having rolled up its sleeves and got its hands dirty it presents itself with proud grit under its fingernails.

The hope is that the grit, properly nurtured, can be turned into pearls.

Each story draws a conclusion, the lesson learnt, and adds it to the list of 'rules.' At the end of each section three killer questions are asked in an attempt to link my experiences with yours.

Inevitably there are many more questions than those posed here, but answering these alone will put you at a considerable advantage over those who don't bother.

Most important of all, it should be fun. It was written with a smile, not an earnest frown, and my biggest hope is that it will be read that way too.

Chapter 1
First things first, what is a Brand?

The word originates from an old Norse word, 'brandr,' meaning 'burnt.' It's of Anglo-Saxon origin and was based on how the Etruscans, Greeks and Romans marked their pottery. It's also how ranchers claimed ownership of their cattle.

As the concept of branding has grown, this simplistic term has led to much confusion, as the word 'Brand' is still too often seen as being about logos and marques. Whilst they're an important part of the process, they're by no means what modern branding is really about.

The game has moved on from simply stamping marks on things.

One school of thought describes a Brand as:

'The value of a business beyond the financial worth of its tangible assets.'

Or, in a word, 'goodwill.'

Something that the City has been applying to the valuations of businesses for years. This might come as something of a shock for the hard-bitten money-men who dismiss branding as 'soft' and 'intangible,' and therefore somehow less valuable.

For my money this definition is a little too accounting-based and a little too manufacturing-led.

Or, in two words, 'old hat.'

The ad-boys have also had a go at defining it, inevitably. And, equally inevitably, it's short and snappy:

'Product + Personality = Brand.'

Not bad, but I've heard it described as 'deeply shallow' by unkind observers.

Also not bad is this crowd-pleaser:

'Brand = Promises Delivered.'

If your business extends a promise that is consistently met, it'll grow to become a trusted Brand. Hard to argue with, but still not, in my view, the whole story.

The stories in this book made me refine and re-define my understanding of what a Brand is, and how branding works. The final chapters deal with this in detail, but the short version is that Brands are inside-out creatures.

They have to have discovered their essential Truth – their 'Single Organising Principle.' And, having done so, they allow their Single Organising Principle to govern the three most important areas of their owner's business:

- its **Culture,**
- its **Products (or Service),**
- its **Reputation.**

The consistent application of the Single Organising Principle across these three areas means the business will be better aligned, more focused, more efficient and ultimately more profitable.

So a Brand by my reckoning is a Single Organising Principle brought to life coherently, continuously and consistently.

It means that every single thing the business does is 'branded,' and it does it in its own unique way.

But more of that later. Here are the stories.

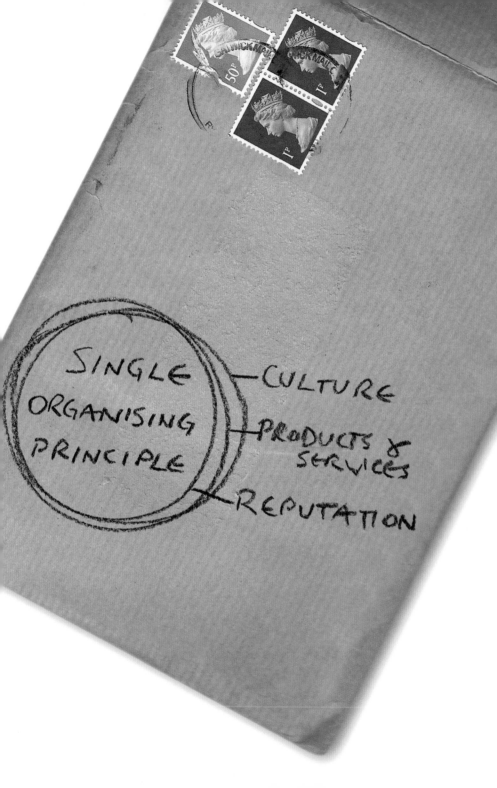

NOTES:

What is a Brand?

1. How you would personally define what a Brand is?

2. Which of the earlier definitions fits your current circumstances best?

Why?

3. Does your organisation use or have you heard other definitions?

What are they?

MORE NOTES

Chapter 2
1978; life below the apples and pears

My first job, in September '78, was with Benton & Bowles, an American-owned advertising agency at 197 Knightsbridge, in London. My title was 'Production Assistant.'

The salary was a princely £2,001.00 per annum. When I asked them what the £1 was for they told me it was in case the computer made a mistake and awarded me the monthly equivalent of the full £20k.

I've always thought that was unnecessarily mean-spirited of them.

The Production Department was responsible for getting print materials to the newspapers in the right format, at the right time. It was staffed by seven broad Cockneys and headed by Bill Jones, an incongruously neat and tidy yet barrel-chested man, with dainty hands and nimble feet who, had he been a rugby player, would have been a scrum-half.

My job was to clear out and manage the old artwork store in the basement of the building. Their well-worn gag about working in the bowels of Benton & Bowles wasn't lost on me and I set about it with a youthful earnest intent.

"donnez-moi une fracture, Bill, I'm sur la valise."

I learnt more Cockney rhyming slang in my short time there than I've ever heard since and, of course, was sent out for the obligatory tins of elbow grease and left-handed screw-drivers; a challenge at the best of times, but made worse in the middle of Knightsbridge…

But they didn't teach me just Cockney rhyming slang. They weren't averse to a little Franglais too. The standard response to an instruction from Bill was to reassure him that they were on the case with a cheery "OK Bill, I'm sur la valise."

Alternatively, when a little less inclined to please him they would ask him to "donnez-moi une fracture," meaning, for those like me who needed it translated, 'give me a break.'

The sport of winding up a fresh-faced 18-year old public school ex-Headboy was ceaseless and I had to learn fast. Being referred to as 'Boy' wasn't helpful, not least because I hadn't been far off 'Sir' only a few brief months earlier.

The predominant culture was 'work hard, play hard,' and whilst they didn't do much of the former, they were spectacularly good at the latter. It was all based around the pub, and provoked by the endless visits of various suppliers who would arrive with predictable regularity at 12.30 or 5.30 – or both.

I have never known so much beer consumed and, to their eternal credit, I was forbidden from paying for a single pint in all my time there.

Despite the casual dress of the department I insisted on turning up in a suit and tie every day even though much of the work was physical and dirty. It was an inverted form of rebellion and a handrail I would cling to as I started to find my feet in this new grown-up world.

Inadvertently I'd learnt an early and important lesson about branding, personal or otherwise: work out who you are, what you stand for, stick to it come what may, and always, always look the part.

It's as true for people as it is for businesses. Maybe it was just another way of trying to be different.

It wasn't really a proper job, but it was a real break and I was now swimming within the system. Either way, they were diamond geezers, every one of them.

NOTES

1. What was your first exposure to Brands and branding?

Was it recently, or a surprisingly long time ago?

2. What's your own personal Brand?

3. If you've worked out what you stand for, to what extent do you 'stick to it come what may, and always, always, look the part'?

MORE NOTES

Chapter 3
1981; the psychology of peas

After a short spell at a company that sadly no longer exists, Lonsdales,
I joined SSC&B:Lintas in New Fetter Lane just off Fleet Street in 1981.
I considered this one to be my first proper job.

It was a well-established traditional agency with a lot of Unilever business.
In those days experience with 'fmcg' (fast moving consumer goods) was
considered important for the cv, so I had done well to have landed a serious
job so quickly into my career.

I was 21 and rather full of myself.

On visiting the Planning Director's office one afternoon I noticed a document
on his desk, about as thick as a Phonebook. But it was the title that caught my
attention: 'The Psychology of Frozen Peas.'

Having navigated my way through the Cockney waters of Benton & Bowles
I was just coming to terms with the psychology of human beings. To be
confronted with the concept that peas might have one of their own was as
weird as it was wonderful.

On reading it I came to understand that this was a defence document, advising
Birds Eye on how to protect their market share, and margin no doubt, from
the incursion of a growing threat – the supermarkets' 'own label.' It focused
on research that showed that mothers were particularly concerned about what
they fed their children, and that Birds Eye could be in a position to capitalise
on this insight by de-positioning the own label offerings as inferior.

By implication, serving up anything other than the accepted best meant falling
short in your motherly duties.

Or, put another way, a guilt trip.

After a brief moral gulp it started to become clear to me; they *were* the best, I'd been to the East Anglian fields and seen them 'picked and frozen in two and a half hours,' and they'd pioneered the market. Nobody else was doing this, and they deserved the credit for it.

More importantly for me, they provided me with the first of the nine and a half golden rules:

Rule 1

Your ● Brand isn't an optional extra; it's a genuinely powerful competitive weapon.

The stronger the Brand, the higher and thicker the walls of the fortress that defends your business.

Just ask Unilever what the jolly Captain Birds Eye did for their fish fingers.

And it's not just true for fmcg; it's also true for business-to-business.

NOTES

Your Brand isn't an optional extra; it's a genuinely powerful competitive weapon.

1. What is your organisation's current attitude towards branding? Disdain? Ignorance? Ill-informed interest? Or a sincere belief that it represents the future of the enterprise?

2. What level of support within the organisation is there for investing in it systematically, like there might be investment in training, corporate entertainment or capital equipment? What would the FD say? What would the Board say? What would the staff say?

3. Do any of your competitors use their Brand well as a competitive weapon? What can be learnt from them?

MORE NOTES

Chapter 4
1983; getting it wrong, by numbers

"A principle isn't a principle until it costs you money."

Lintas and Bird's Eye taught me well, in an old-school way, but it was time to move on. I was a young man in a hurry and having done a couple of years learning the stodgy discipline of good Client service I wanted to balance the cv with something more creative.

Doyle Dane Bernbach, another American agency, was world-famous for its creative work, especially its Volkswagen advertising. It had been founded by Bill Bernbach, a genius by any measure, and was now being run by his son John.

Bill, as John was to find out, was a hard act to follow.

Bill had given the world some wise and simple soundbites, my favourites being "a principle isn't a principle until it costs you money," and "nothing kills a bad product quicker than good advertising." The latter has multi-applications and, not satisfied with merely stealing it, I also had the gall to bend it to suit my purposes. So, it also works as 'nothing kills a bad idea quicker than good publicity.' I hope he forgives me.

I've passed them on to my children.

I was hired by Philip Gould, later to become Lord Gould, Tony Blair's chief pollster. He was slight and lithe, with a quick mind and a gait that made him glide when he walked. He moved in short, sudden bursts in a way that only high-energy people do, and wore a permanent look of bemusement on his face, as though watching proceedings rather than directing them.

Philip was a misfit there and I think he was looking for a kindred spirit. In those terms, he'd found one.

On my first day they had a small celebration for the opening of a new wing in the building in Baker Street where I was to be housed. It was all clinking champagne glasses and very civilised but I remember a cold, draining feeling as the 'guests' left our new wing and I was alone with my new office and the people who were part of the team I had joined.

I had made a terrible mistake.

I didn't belong here at all. There was nobody I had an affinity with, other than maybe Philip, and he was miles away on the other side of the building. I couldn't go running there every five minutes for camaraderie. Now what?

Oh dear.

One of the Clients I was assigned to was Heinz Tomato Ketchup, a highly prestigious assignment in ad-land.

You can imagine the Agency's consternation on receipt of the news that Heinz were considering introducing a new squeezable bottle. 'Now hang on,' went the Baker Street cry. 'We've spent years and millions educating the great British public that Heinz is the slow ketchup, with dozens of catchy commercials with jolly truckers, kids and grannies all bashing away at the bottom of the glass jar to induce their favourite sauce to dollop lovingly onto their fish and chips, pie and peas or sausage and mash. You can't possibly change the jar,' we continued hysterically, 'you'll ruin everything.'

Heinz didn't listen, pressed on with their plans and, of course, it was a roaring success.

It led me to the second golden rule:

rule 2

Get the proposition right. It probably isn't what you think it is.

Heinz's real proposition wasn't about the jar at all. It was about meal enhancement. 'Slow,' or 'squeezable' were simply delivery mechanisms for the goodies inside. Making the food taste better was always the real proposition, regardless of delivery mechanism. Convenient packaging was an added feature.

Some years later when I had my first business I came across this example with a vacuum cleaning business called VAX. The CEO, Patrick Austen, had been the CEO at Liberty, that great temple of retail eclecticism who we'd described as 'Purveyors of the Idiosyncratic since 1875.' He knew that VAX hadn't really got to their most potent proposition so he asked us to have a look.

VAX's stock in trade had been its fantastic cleaning capabilities. The machines had terrific engines that not only washed carpets and floors but also vacuumed them. And they were flexible, so you didn't have to go through the whole wash-and-dry hassle every time you just wanted a quick 'hoover-up.' So why wouldn't you want one? (It's OK, even they accepted that it's impossible to talk about this market without mentioning the H-word).

Our research quickly established that their machines were indeed the best of their sort, but we equally quickly uncovered something more exciting.

What was really going on with these potential consumers was an enactment of the cliché 'Tidy home, tidy mind.'

The tidying of the home is as much to signal to the world and oneself that 'I'm in control and haven't gone mad' as it is to genuinely hanker after tidiness *per se*.

That's why so many women will confess to having a frantic tidy-up before the cleaning lady comes round. They know that the cleaner is going to see every dark corner of the house and therefore expose whatever madness might be lurking there.

It's the most logical piece of ill-logic I've come across.

So we moved VAX from thinking that their proposition was about 'Cleaning floors,' to their real proposition, which was about 'Brightening homes.' The deep-down cleaning of the carpets became a relative irrelevance; these people wanted 'visible clean – fast.' Powerful engines were much more useful to them as agents for achieving 'visible clean – fast,' rather than 'deep-down clean,' as they had been positioned previously.

We suggested that they needed two ranges: one domestic, and one industrial (where 'cleaning' was always going to remain important). Same technologies, different propositions.

When it came to another Client, Homebase, we suggested they stop thinking of themselves as a 'DIY shed,' and start thinking of themselves as a 'home-making shop' instead. It was based on an understanding that their shopper profile showed a higher incidence of couples shopping together compared with the relatively more hairy-arsed profile of the B&Qs and other 'builder-related' offerings.

It was a fundamentally different proposition and, importantly, one they've owned to this day with 'Make a house a home.'

It also led them to agree a concession deal with Laura Ashley. Not the sort of concession that would have gone down so well in B&Q or Wickes.

My time at Doyle Dane Bernbach was pretty miserable. The agency was losing its way, I didn't get on with the other people (Philip had long gone), Heinz turned out to be a company that was producing advertising by numbers – literally – with ridiculous research techniques that measured commercials second by second, forcing us into work that was all head and no heart, and making us make changes we didn't believe in.

To cap it all, my mother was diagnosed with terminal cancer and given six months to live.

I was there 18 months but it felt like one long, dark winter. It was time for a new start.

NOTES
Get the proposition right. It probably isn't what you think it is.

1. Are you able to deliver your Brand's 'elevator pitch?' Without a hint of embarrassment? What about the Board? All of them?

2. Is it based on a customer or consumer insight?

3. Is it uniquely true to you, your product or service? Have you analysed your competitors properly and found sustainable, 'clear-blue' differences?

Chapter 5
1985; the highs at Lowe's

'Canada; gentle giant of the North'

Lowe Howard-Spink was an agency founded by one of the industry's original 'enfants terribles,' Frank Lowe, now Sir Frank.

He was famous for an unbridled passion for high quality creative work, a generous collection of cricket jumpers, and an irascible temper. To me he was God-like. His long curly sandy hair, a disdainful air and a prowling feline slouch all added up to making him a dangerous man to know. But how exciting.

The offices were again in Knightsbridge but this time, mercifully, basement-free. In fact, they overlooked Hyde Park and were stunning. He had imported Italian mosaic flooring, the loos were carved mahogany with antique-style oversized urinals, with individual deep and fluffy blue hand-towels - the exact colour-match with the Corporate colours – collected in matching woven baskets, refreshed daily.

I was to work for Peter Stephenson-Wright, more commonly known, as it transpired, as Peter Stephenson-Wrong. He left the day I started so I have no way of knowing who was right and who was wrong.

Instead I had the good fortune to end up working for Sean O'Connor, an urbane, tall and witty Irishman with a keen eye for fun. He had piercing turquoise eyes set in a slightly tired face and a mouth that was permanently poised for laughter. He was one of those people you look at and smile, expecting a joke. I'm sure he could have made just as good a living from being a professional dinner party guest on account of his storytelling skills.

One of his favourite pastimes was to compete with friends to see who could find the dullest newspaper headline. He told me one day that whilst he was sad to only come second in that month's competition, he was happy to concede graciously to the worthy winner: 'Canada; gentle giant of the North.'

One of the soundest pieces of advice he gave me was on the happy day I declared that I was getting married. Without so much as a pause to offer congratulations and all the other platitudes that men find so difficult in these situations, he got up from his sofa and walked round to sit behind his desk. Leaning forward he said, in his most avuncular tone, "Bertie, there's just one thing you need to realise. It's not your wedding. Nor hers. It's her mother's."

How right he was. I've passed it on often.

I was working on the GM Vauxhall account. Frank had bought the agency that previously had the business so that he could get his hands on it. Inevitably, there was a culture clash.

This made for a difficult relationship between the agency and the Client but there was plenty to do and it was our biggest Client. Our objective was to get them to run work that was as famous as some of Lowe's other Clients, including 'Heineken refreshes the parts that other beers can't reach,' and Stella's 'Reassuringly Expensive' campaign.

In an internal meeting one morning I found myself engaged in a debate that opened up a whole new and exciting world of Brand possibilities. The argument was about whether or not we should be persuading GM to invest their money behind a Brand campaign as opposed to supporting each of the models individually.

The logic was that there's a 'cascade' to how people buy cars, starting with 'I'd like a Vauxhall,' then 'maybe the Astra,' then 'maybe the 1.4,' then 'maybe a blue one.'

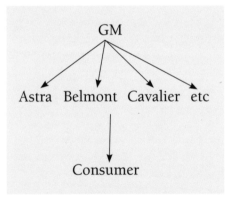 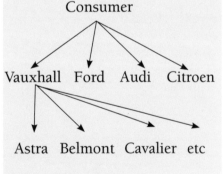

GM communications structure   How people buy cars

I realised that I was being drawn increasingly fervently towards this logic and that I was making a stand on the difference between the internal structure of a Company and the external presentation of its Brand. I was supported in that view by Alfredo Marcantonio, the then Creative Director, author of many famous Volkswagen advertisements and proud son of an Italian ice-cream seller. He was to become a friend and significant figure in my future.

It was a layer of complexity that I hadn't encountered before and it meant grappling with concepts like Master-Brands, sub-Brands and Brand Architecture. The plot thickened. It was a deeper discussion, more grown-up, more meaningful, and much more exciting.

It led to the running of 'Vauxhall: once driven, forever smitten,' and taught me a third important lesson in this 'golden rules' trail:

rule 3

The company structure shouldn't define your Brand; your Brand should define the company structure.

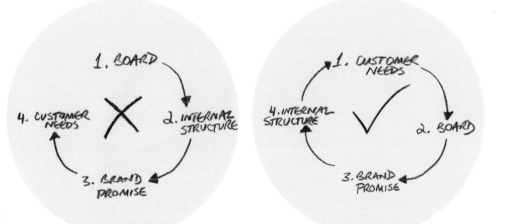

Vauxhall struggled with the notion for a while. Their communications were structured around how they made the cars, not around how people bought them. But, to their credit, they did accept the logic in the end.

More recently I was advising Lawrie Haynes, the then CEO of the telecomms arm of Lattice plc on his Brand. Lawrie's a big and big-picture man, and an outstanding leader. People can't help but like working for him because he genuinely knows how to delegate responsibility, something that so many CEOs seem to find so difficult.

I've been the happy recipient of his favourite delegation advice more than once, most memorably on the occasion when I was asked to deliver a major speech at his first Conference as the new CEO. Having made the most flattering and eulogistic of introductions, he smiled broadly and warmly as I rose to climb the steps to meet him on stage to deliver my speech. Against the background of the noise of clapping, he extended his hand and, still beaming, leant forward and said "Don't fuck it up…"

It's advice I've seen him give to senior directors and subordinates charged with important projects alike. We all know what he means.

On concluding my recommendations in a meeting months later, he looked up over his glasses and said "an hour ago, when you started, I had a very clear idea about who my top three acquisition targets were. And number one was easily ahead of the pack. Now you've finished, number two is by far the better prospect. The culture clash of going with number one will produce carnage. Our Brand and number two's Brand are a much better fit."

I could have hugged him.

To hear the CEO of a major organisation using his Brand to define and shape the future structure of his business was music to my ears. It struck me as a much more visionary, purposeful and enlightened form of leadership.

At last, people were beginning to see just how powerful this could be.

Lawrie and I have worked together twice since, including during his spell as CEO of The British Nuclear Group. He had always said he only wanted to work within organisations that had 'costly, controversial or complex' problems.

BNG provided him with a hat-trick. But he's scored again recently against these criteria, as the newly appointed 'President, Nuclear,' at Rolls-Royce.

When I joined Lowe Howard-Spink there were 23 of us. By the time I left, three years later, there were over 120 people. The success was in no small part due to the presence of Tim Bell.

He too has since been elevated to the House of Lords.

His easy manner and twinkle in the eye captured a golden time for me, no better than one Friday evening when a number of us were gathered in my shared office with the television on and several cases of Stella and Heineken being sampled. Tim appeared at the door, in a suit but with no shoes on, and enquired what was going on.

"Not much," we replied. "Usual Friday evening gathering. What's going on with you?"

"Oh, bankers' meeting," he said wearily. "It's so dull I had to leave and go for a little wander before I go back. I'd rather be in here with you lot."

At which point, across the crowded room, I asked him if he could confirm a piece of industry folklore, which suggested that the legendary charm of Tim Bell was such that dogs would cross the street to be stroked by him.

"Oh yes," he twinkled, immediately. "But unfortunately it used to be girls."

He was always a great showman. Even in his socks.

I left Lowe Howard-Spink with Geoff Howard-Spink's timeless advice in my ears: "Bertie, remember, reasonable men don't change the world."

He was that kind of man and it was that kind of place.

But he was right.

"Remember, reasonable men don't change the world."

NOTES

The company structure shouldn't define your Brand; your Brand should define the company structure.

1. Is your organisation structured for administrative convenience, or to deliver a better product or service?

2. Does the current structure reflect and support the Brand promise?

3. When re-structures are talked about within your organisation, does the Brand play any part in helping inform decisions? Can you see how it could?

Chapter 6
1988; the Ultimate Branding Machine

1988, Thatcher's Britain.

In Wall Street they were saying that 'greed is good,' and that 'lunch is for wimps.'

Not agreeing with either statement, my strategy for coping with these prevailing attitudes was to combine them by enjoying a series of greedy lunches with a range of interesting people.

The economic times allowed for it…

Thatcher's Britain was characterised by Norman Tebbit's response to the three million unemployed his Party had inherited: "on yer bike." It encouraged self-starters and entrepreneurs and this was most evident in the quality of graduate cvs that we were receiving. It was particularly marked from one year to the next when, instead of receiving cvs full of stories of how they'd followed the hippy trail in India in their gap year, they'd started businesses instead. They'd all cut their hair and put suits on, and it was clear that we were in a new era.

"Those were the days, my friend, we thought they'd never end…" lamented the Mary Hopkin song from the sixties. The same is true for the '80s, but in a very different way.

I was now at WCRS or, to do it its full glorious justice, WCRS Mathews Marcantonio. My life had changed dramatically after a phone call from Marcantonio. He had left Lowe's and was trying to build a new team at WCRS. He wanted people around him that he knew and trusted. Flattered by the phone call I was delighted to go and see him in his new office in Covent Garden.

We drank a couple of Carling Black labels out of loyalty to one of their Clients and the owner of the famous 'I bet he drinks Carling Black label' campaign, and reminisced about our time at Lowe's before he came out with what it was he was really after.

I'm looking for someone to come and work on the BMW business.'

I wanted to splutter into my beer but it was a good moment to escape to the loo to muster some composure.

In Brand terms I'd hit the jackpot.

BMW was recognised as one of those Clients you dream of working with, especially at that time.

WCRS had built their reputation on it and the work, based on founder Robin Wight's philosophy of 'interrogate the product until it confesses to its strengths,' was rightly regarded around the world as some of the finest in history.

The Brand was one of the great icons of the '80s, a product built for winners, by winners.

It was a privilege to be invited into such exalted circles and the scale of the opportunity was obvious to me straight away.

There was no need for further conversation. We agreed everything we needed to and I left for home bursting with excitement at the way things had turned out.

I started there as soon as I could and shortly after was provided with a new BMW 535i, referred to, with feeling, as 'The Red Throbber.' At the age of 28 I found myself on the WCRS Board.

In the midst of their 'winning culture,' BMW had invested in sponsoring Touring Car racing. With their usual impeccable timing, television coverage of the sport was rising fast so they caught it at exactly the right time. Predictably, as the ink on the contract was still drying, the BMW-sponsored vehicles started to win everything.

One Monday morning late in the season, after a particularly successful racing weekend, I was in a meeting with Tom Purves, BMW's Managing Director. He was of Scottish Presbyterian extract, pristine neat, with a fiercely straight back, ruddy cheeks and immaculate tightly-knotted wavy hair. A man of great manners, and deep and genuine integrity for whom I had towering respect. As he arrived for the meeting I, flushed with enthusiasm for the weekend's track exploits, blurted out "Tom, what a weekend! We're winning everything; isn't it great?"

"Actually," he replied, ever cool, "I'm slightly alarmed."

That made me alarmed. What could possibly be bothering him about this seemingly endless parade of victories featuring his own products, in front of millions of people who had tuned into a sport that he'd just sponsored at a fraction of the price of its true worth? I was sure he had his reasons, but at that moment they were beyond me.

"Oh yes?" I asked, a bit taken aback. "Why's that?"

"Well," he said, "as the competition at these events becomes more fierce the drivers are bumping into each other more and more. Bits are flying off the cars. It's becoming stock car racing. I'm alarmed at how much harm our association with all this could be doing to the Brand. I think we should pull out altogether."

And then his immortal words,

"We can win in our own way."

I was stunned. First at his response, and then at the realisation of his innate sense of diligent and thoughtful Brand management. I had a new understanding of the adage that not all publicity is good publicity.

I didn't realise it at the time but Tom's words were to become the backbone of my belief in Brands and the process of branding. They were a huge leap in the 'Know Thyself' trail, and they also provided me with the fourth lesson:

rule 4

Branding is about winning in your own way.

Successful Brands, like people, win on their own terms. BMW were masters of this; self-determining, clear of purpose, brave and, above all, true to themselves.

They were governed by a laser-like focus on their Brand and what it stood for. If it didn't amplify 'The Ultimate Driving Machine' then it wasn't done. Full stop.

No time-wasting, no politically motivated initiatives, no misguided debates and no prisoners. You either got it or you got out of the way.

And that is exactly as it should be.

BMW's mastery of their subject was such that they also re-defined my understanding of Marketing.

Seeing the designers at their easels in Munich, calculating which shade of orange for the dials would be easiest on the eye, or planning the layout of the instrumentation so that it fell within easy reach of a stretched hand, or calibrating the angle of the wrap-around cockpit to deliver the 'ultimate driving position,' all made me realise that, as they were doing it, they had the market right there, firmly in mind, on those easels. It wasn't design for its own sake, or vanity, it was Marketing in action; using market knowledge to produce market-driven products.

Or, put another way, providing drivers with 'The Ultimate Driving machine.'

They are living proof that at the heart of every powerful Brand is an outstanding product.

It's a global truism, one that defeats the cynical, the lazy and the incompetent who try to hide behind spin or what Philip Bowman, previous CEO of Allied Domecq and now CEO of Smiths calls "a tissue of deceit."

'Winning in your own way' is the essence of powerful Branding. It's what differentiates the champions from the cheats.

In discussion about this with Brent Hoberman, founder of lastminute.com, he recounted a story from Charles Dunstone, founder of Carphone Warehouse.

In Charles' own words: "simply put, if you're first to do something new for customers, customers believe you did it for them. If you copy something someone else has already done for customers, customers believe you did it for yourself."

'Winning in your own way' is a philosophy that forces an organisation to follow its own heart, to be true to itself. Brent Hoberman and Charles Dunstone are living examples of people who have embraced this. And they've built big, powerful and valuable Brands on the back of it.

And around the world BMW continues to stand tall as a beacon of how to win in your own way.

NOTES

Branding is about winning in your own way.

1. Are you clear about what 'your way' is? Are others?

2. As a culture, do you collectively follow your own rules of what's right and wrong, or do you tend to respond to market and competitive movement?

3. Are you jealous of whoever does this well in your sector? Just how jealous?

MORE NOTES

Chapter 7
1990; it's always good to talk.

In the milky sunlight streaming through the tall windows of an office off Fleet Street overlooking the River Thames, the air was thick with purple cigar smoke. In this office a presentation had just come to an end.

I wasn't there but the results of this meeting were to inform the next four years of my life.

They would also alter BT's fortunes.

At the meeting there were a number of confused faces around the table, with two exceptions. One was the man who had just delivered his recommendations, Norman Strauss, an outstanding Brand strategist, and generator of the cigar smoke. He was a professor-like figure whose front door at home where he worked needed to be pushed hard to get past the stack of old newspapers gathering dust in the corridor.

The other was BT's Director of Communications, Adrian Hosford, who in time would become my boss, mentor and friend.

After months of intensive work Norman had triumphantly informed the team of senior BT executives that they weren't really in the business of telephones, nor were they in the business of exploiting the country's largest installer base, and nor even were they in the technology business.

They were, in fact, in the business of 'Reciprocated Confidences...'

Little surprise there was confusion. It was later to confuse me too.

In my time at WCRS I had been part of a team that had pitched for the BT account. It would be a significant victory if we won it, not least because it was viewed internally as an outward sign that the agency was growing up and could compete with the big boys.

We did win it. And so my long relationship with Adrian began.

He was another Irishman with a ready smile, a gentle manner and a wicked glint in his eye. He was a maverick in the big corporate system because he was brave, visionary and a wilful breaker of rules.

Over 18 months as a Client of WCRS, Adrian and I developed a good working and personal relationship. One evening, enjoying a drink together in his office, he shocked me by asking if I'd ever consider coming to work with him at BT.

"But you'd never have anywhere for me to park my car," I responded facetiously, "and, anyway, why would I want to come and work with a load of people who wear grey plastic shoes?"

"Oh, I think we could sort something out about the car," he said, rightly ignoring the insulting banality of the shoe remark.

"You're not serious, are you?" I carried on, suddenly sensing that he wasn't just flirting.

"Well," he said, "I think it would do you a lot of good to spread your wings and see life from the buyer's perspective, not just the seller's."

It was an awkward moment because I knew he was right. But I hadn't come over that evening to change jobs, leave aside provoke such a dramatic change.

I'd never worked outside the advertising arena, I'd never worked in a company of more than 150 people, and I'd always considered myself as the expert who gave the advice, not the Client who bought it.

"Well I don't think you're really serious about it and I really can't see how it would ever work," I blustered, rather wanting to change the subject as I had to admit that his left hook had hit me hard and was making me wobble.

The overnight test revealed what had started to become evident the previous evening. My inner voice was telling me that I should just shut my eyes and jump. The fact that it had recently been voted 'Britain's Most Hated Company,' coupled with consistent stories in the newspapers detailing the Chairman's 'outrageous' salary, only added to the sense of madness.

So I did indeed jump the Client/ agency fence and join BT, sporting the self-important title 'Worldwide Head of Advertising and Media Quality.'

BT had 250,000 people and a communications budget of £120m.

And I was a precocious 32-year old.

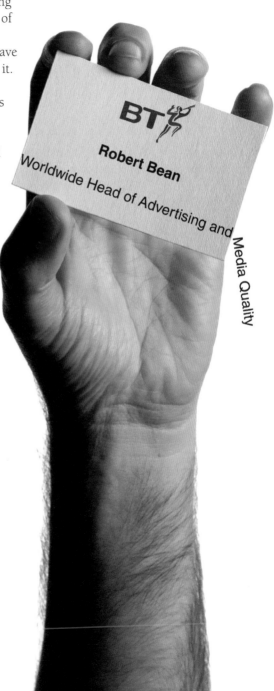

Adrian did sort out my car, they didn't wear grey plastic shoes, and I was about to discover just how many industry friends I never knew I had.

And so to a rather ordinary meeting room one Thursday morning, when Adrian was presenting from a 4x5ft wall chart. In the chart was a complex grid of boxes, each one containing a letter and number code. It looked like a Sudoku/Crossword pile-up, and proved to be just as unintelligible.

He patiently explained the significance of each box, and the significance of the contents of each box, but I could tell his audience, including me, just wasn't with him. Undeterred, he pressed on, with mounting enthusiasm, until he breathlessly reached what was to him the only incontrovertible, inevitable and natural conclusion to his feverish exertions... "reciprocated confidences."

I felt like applauding, but it would have been fraudulent.

I looked across the room to see if it was just me who was bewildered and was gratified to see that the Planning Director of Saatchi and Saatchi, Rita Clifton, a woman whose high intellect and common sense were of equal measure, was shuffling her papers as if preparing to leave, studiously avoiding looking up lest she, like the rest of us, was found out.

As we left the meeting others in the department asked what it had been about. Rita muttered something about 'reciprocated trousers' and we all rushed off to pick up our phone messages.

Over the next year, these two words, 'reciprocated confidences,' took up a lot of my life. I still couldn't say I understood them properly but the notions around them were becoming clearer and the fog was lifting slowly.

Sensing that his top team needed more coaching in this area, Adrian arranged a four-day away session for the five of us. It was to be facilitated by Dr Nick Georgiades, an industrial psychologist and previous Director of HR at British Airways during their famous period of change. He was a deeply passionate and profound man who endeared himself to me instantly when he kicked off proceedings by declaring that our purpose over the next four days was to re-interpret 'reciprocated confidences' so that staff up and down the Company could share the thinking and "have a vision of the cathedral whilst they mix the cement."

It struck me as a noble purpose.

On a break in the middle of day two, Adrian and I were walking across the front lawn of the Bath Spa Hotel. We were lost in conversation.

He was telling me that he was one of six children, born on a farm in west Cork, and that his sisters in particular had helped raise him. He talked a lot about his family and I listened intently for what Nick Georgiades had described as "the music, not just the words."

Then it was my turn. I told him about being born in Brazil and the trauma of moving to England when I was 12. And about my English father and Italian mother who was Catholic and, as sinners go, had been a pretty good role model. I carried on, uninvited and without pause, about details that had shaped my life.

In the middle of these intimate rantings, the penny dropped.

We were reciprocating our own confidences.

It all suddenly made sense. The exchange of 'confidences' was leading to better communications between us and, in turn, deepening our relationship. What a big, brilliant and simple thought. Norman and Adrian were right: BT really wasn't about the telephone exchange or the installer base or technology; they really could be about improving relationships through enabling the 'reciprocation of confidences.'

Reciprocating confidences:
a little known fact about BT's piper logo was that the piper is listening as well as broadcasting.

It was a visionary and market-leading thought. They'd managed to redefine communications, the very premise on which BT ran, and they'd put their arms around it to claim it as their own.

Quite an important discovery for the phone company.

This was my epiphany. The power in what was ultimately such a simple thought was electrifying. It brought the whole process of branding to a new level, one that was going to be the foundations of my future. The depth of understanding of emotion and psychology, matched with the breadth of application that this idea clearly had, was as transformational for me as it turned out to be for BT.

In the months that followed we brought 'reciprocated confidences' to life by making the famous corporate TV commercial featuring Stephen Hawking. The objective was to interpret the two words in a way that would be meaningful for the staff, now reduced to a mere 150,000.

The script read:

FOR MILLIONS OF YEARS MANKIND LIVED LIKE THE ANIMALS.

THEN SOMETHING HAPPENED WHICH UNLEASHED THE POWER

OF OUR IMAGINATION.

WE LEARNT TO TALK.

WE LEARNT TO LISTEN.

SPEECH HAS ALLOWED THE COMMUNICATION OF IDEAS

ENABLING HUMAN BEINGS TO WORK TOGETHER - TO BUILD

THE IMPOSSIBLE.

MANKIND'S GREATEST ACHIEVEMENTS HAVE COME ABOUT

BY TALKING -

AND ITS GREATEST FAILURES BY NOT TALKING.

IT DOESN'T HAVE TO BE LIKE THIS.

OUR GREATEST HOPES CAN BECOME REALITY IN THE FUTURE.

WITH THE TECHNOLOGY AT OUR DISPOSAL THE POSSIBILITIES

ARE UNBOUNDED.

ALL WE NEED TO DO IS MAKE SURE WE KEEP TALKING,

TALKING, TALKING, TALKING, TALKING.

The claim at the end was no bigger than 'BT is helping to keep the world talking.'

The effect was revolutionary. It made the staff see themselves in quite a different way. The van drivers were no longer 'just' van drivers, and the telephonists were no longer 'just' telephonists. They were now helping to keep the world talking, not an insignificant responsibility…

In time, it would be sent to Tony Blair on the eve of the historic Northern Irish peace talks as a way of supporting his strategy to 'keep talking' with Gerry Adams.

But it was time to make 'reciprocated confidences' meaningful for consumers too. In the big showpiece pitch that followed, David Abbot and his agency AMV won the business in a performance from David that was as good as any thespian or political leader.

His response to the briefing document that had taken months to prepare and was measurable by its weight, running as it did to several inches deep, was four simple but unforgettable words: 'It's good to talk.'

Not satisfied with the brilliant simplicity of the line, he also wrapped up the whole campaign by employing Bob Hoskins to deliver it in his inimitable tough and macho Cockney style.

'It's good to talk.'

David's brilliance at condensing such complexities into four seemingly innocuous words made me re-think the true nature of creativity.

In both cases, with scientific Stephen Hawking and bruiser Bob Hoskins, we had people either unable to, or not known for their ability to communicate, celebrating the virtues of communication. It had a wonderful circular inner logic.

The facts speak for themselves; that campaign delivered BT an incremental £5bn over the five years it ran, an astonishing result and true testament to the power of good communications.

David's brilliance at condensing such complexities into four seemingly innocuous words made me re-think the true nature of creativity. The common perception of creativity is that it is an expansionist process, with the artist adding layer on layer of depth and subtlety, ultimately creating something of such profundity and wonder that we, the creatively stifled, can do little more than marvel at it. And that's exciting when it happens.

But I want to make the case for the reductivist.

That brutal, ruthless, editorially-minded, scythe-wielding seeker of the Fundamental Truth. The absorber, stripper, truncater and reconstituter of information that was previously confusing for the rest of us yet, in his studied grasp, is reduced into something not just meaningful but motivating too. What an act of equal creative genius. What a woefully under appreciated, under acknowledged and under-valued form of creativity.

Another reductivist in this marketplace is Ratheesh Yoganathan. He's the founder and CEO of Lebara Mobile, provider of low-cost international SIM cards for ethnic migrants living away from their families. He was very clear about how he sees the value of his product: "For me it's like this, Robert. In life there's only air, water and phone your Mum."

He's the same reductivist who, when asked what single cultural value he rated the highest among his staff answered, unhesitatingly, that it was their ability to "feel the customer."

It's a €200m business.

He's 33.

Reductivism works.

Learnings from 'reciprocated confidences' and BT have informed how I've approached every branding task since, and they also provided the fifth step on the learning trail:

rule 5

To have great communications you first need to understand 'reciprocating confidences.'

At the heart of the idea of 'reciprocated confidences' is the belief that communications can only be successful if they're truly two-way. I still bristle at the wastage of so much bad communication. Annual reports, websites, e-mails, ads and more, that merely tell or simply cajole. Businesses that don't understand this fundamental principle are missing real opportunities at best and, at worst, giving their smarter rivals an unfair advantage.

Despite stringent market regulation for over 20 years BT still doesn't have a major competitor in the UK. And that hasn't come about by chance.

NOTES

To have great communications you first need to understand 'reciprocating confidences.'

1. What is your organisation's real view of communications? Is it an expensive 'necessary evil,' or an important strategic tool?

2. Do your communications really empathise with, and genuinely motivate, the audiences they're intended for, whether internal or external?

3. Are they measured accordingly, or just by cost?

But there was a lot more to this experience than the production of great communications.

Everyone in the company who had any kind of contact with customers was trained on how to improve their communication skills. Suddenly operators sounded human and BT started to develop and express its personality. Soon enough it even lost its infamous 'Britain's Most Hated' company tag.

This whole achievement was only possible through the commitment, determination and relentlessness of Adrian, and this taught me a vital sixth lesson:

rule 6

Great Brands need great humans to champion them.

Nowadays before accepting any assignment from a Client I look for two things: firstly, does the brief come from the CEO or equivalent? And secondly, where is the 'Great Human' who will champion the cause?

Sometimes the 'Great Human' is obvious.

Clare Blampied, the perennially elegant Managing Director of Saclà, an Italian family-owned pasta sauce company, has built a £35m business in the UK from scratch, virtually single-handedly.

They are the pioneers of pesto in the UK, and in foodie circles the Saclà product is widely credited to be of oustanding quality.

But she's in the process of building an even greater Brand.

A combination of dazzling charm, a deep and wide knowledge of her subject, profound integrity and a healthy 'jfdi' (just f****** do it) approach to management have all contributed to her terrific success story.

But it's her unswerving focus on championing her Brand at every possible opportunity that's really what's kept her and her business thriving.

The family are lucky to have her.

Sometimes the 'Great Human' is less obvious.

When I recently worked with lastminute.com across the Group's Brands, it was acknowledged by the CEO and CMO Europe that the real hero in the process was a young Scotsman called Mark McCulloch. He was fairly junior and had no particular experience in this area.

But his tireless energy, determination and diplomacy skills meant the difference between six clever strategic solutions sitting in a document somewhere, and every single one of their 2,000 people across Europe undergoing an intensive engagement programme so that they could all rally around their Brands with one voice.

It was an exhausting and exhaustive effort but it simply wouldn't have happened without him.

'Great Humans' are vital cogs in the machinery of branding. They're the determined diplomats, promoting a cause. And the beauty is that they can come from anywhere.

NOTES

Great Brands need great humans to champion them.

1. Who are the potential champions in your organisation? Is it you? And/or who else?

2. If they stood up to be counted, what kind of support could they expect to receive? From you? From others?

3. Who are the sceptics? Can they be brought round? Who by?

My time at BT was both formative and informative. There were horror days when I'd go home and literally weep with frustration, but there were also breakthrough days that meant we could really make important things happen. The horror days were marked by petty politicking, turf wars, and people who had too much time on their hands. They could afford to plot and get in the way of progress. I had disdain for them, and sometimes my frustration was overwhelming.

What kept me sane for much of my time there was a story about the late John Harvey-Jones. He was asked an inane question by a reporter: "Mr Harvey-Jones, after 16 years at the helm of ICI, having bought dozens of companies, hired hundreds of people and fired even more, what kept you going?"

After a brief pause his answer was, "I never joined." The Britalian Brazilian outsider in me found this very meaningful.

The BT experience also made me question the role and value of Marketing in business. At a time when it's struggling to be heard in the Boardroom, I can't think of a more powerful role than to be the catalyst for a journey like the one BT took with Reciprocated Confidences. It would place Marketing in the middle of an organisation, drawing together all the disparate parts of the business. Why, so often, do they seem so unable or unwilling to rise to the challenge and capitalise on the opportunity?

Around this time more and more people, including the City and the FT, were beginning to take Brands and branding more seriously. There was increasing recognition that a strong Brand was an intangible asset that could really add tangible value to a balance sheet.

Having seen at first hand the devastating power of a well defined, well expressed and well managed Brand, I was determined to focus exclusively in this area.

So I set about starting my first business to do just that.

Chapter 8

1994; the first solo flight

In a blaze of Trade publicity I opened the doors of a company called BeanMC.

There were four equal partners and we started from the borrowed offices of a company called Lifeboat Matey, friends of one of the partners. We had a room, a telephone, a fax machine and, in a kind gesture, a vase with flowers in it.

There was no financial backing, despite several good offers, including one from a consortium led by the then Chairman of a top five bank, and a senior member of the Rothschild family. In the flush of proprietorial enthusiasm we were confident we would land some business quickly and thereby chose not be indebted to outside investors in the future.

It was late summer and so a slow news period. The media coverage was extremely generous and kept running for a number of weeks after we'd announced our intentions. There were several front pages, editorial leaders in all the important titles, lots of reviews and articles, with comment from a whole range of opinionated parties. It really was a snowstorm and very evidently, it really was a slow news period…

One morning the fax machine whirred and out came what looked to us like an invitation to tender from a local council. It was barely legible and even less intelligible. Having what we considered to be blue-chip backgrounds we weren't overly excited at the prospect of one of our founding Clients being a local council. Our first Client was in fact Virgin Radio, and they were already on board.

Believing the fax to be sent in error we binned it.

Two weeks later we moved to our own offices, now ready, in Brewer Street in Soho. It had undoubtedly been a bordello as it was tall and narrow with plenty of small rooms off the winding and creaking staircase.

Again, the fax turned up, re-sent. No more legible than last time, and no more intelligible. Again, we binned it.

Finally, a third fax appeared, but this time it included a message scrawled across the top, saying insistently 'PLEASE RESPOND TO THIS FAX.' Three attempts, on two different numbers, and now a note of irritation? We thought we'd better have a look.

It seemed like a company asking for a quote for some print work. Not our bag. On closer inspection it was a company looking for a critique of their print work, not a quote.

The company in question was a Danish company called VELUX Windows.

Having replied to them, a further fax arrived. This one advised us that we had been selected as the UK representative company to compete against a French and a German one, for what was to be a pan-European campaign.

In truth we still didn't take it terribly seriously until a few days before the meeting, when we were due to host a delegation of six of their best to come and hear what we had to say.

We searched through their literature and found that it was crammed with rich detail about the quality of their woods and the glass, and even the screws. But there was something confusing about all this. Here was this enormous Brand, one that we'd all heard of and knew about, as did everyone

we'd mentioned it to, and yet none of us had ever even touched one. What could be the magic that made this happen? It didn't seem to us that it could be as rational as being just about the quality of their glass and screws. Were we missing something?

No, we decided. They were.

So we set about trying to define their deeper proposition, their version of 'Reciprocated Confidences.'

At its most fundamental level, a VELUX roof window introduces light to what is otherwise a dead, dark space. This process of dramatic change felt like a much bigger and more engaging area to be mining in. My sense was that if we could sharpen this thinking we'd have something very powerful to sell them.

The presentation date arrived. Seven of them showed up, not six. As they made their way up the three flights of our rickety staircase my first priority was to work out how to seat them all. It was a tiny office and we had two chairs and a three-seat sofa. So that made five. The remaining two had to edge their way onto the arms of the sofa. Perfect. But coffees were awkward

So we began, with me presenting off a slightly tired old flip-chart, until we reached the climax of our thoughts with a chart that said:

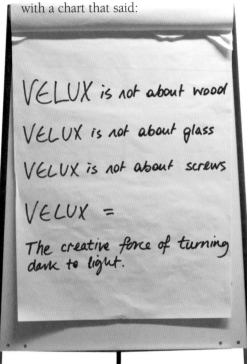

VELUX is not about wood

VELUX is not about glass

VELUX is not about screws

VELUX =

The creative force of turning dark to light.

It was a do or die moment in what was a do or die presentation. Their silence lasted forever.

Then the room exploded. They loved it. They all started talking at once in different languages, eventually asking whether the next meeting should be in Copenhagen or London, and when?

Then someone asked a perfectly reasonable question even if it felt at the time like it was somewhere between cruel and crass: "What International experience do you have?"

As a company that had only been in business for a few months the question brought my elation to near devastation faster than the BMW Red Throbber could get from 0 to 60. I'm reputed to have responded, "Well, my mother was Italian..."

Another pause, and with a few nods and gestures, especially from the Italian representative who now seemed particularly impressed, we were appointed.

They paid us very well, the commercial ran in nine countries across Europe and our company was airborne.

This experience gave me the seventh golden rule:

rule 7

Don't believe that branding is an exclusive club for the rich and beautiful.

A PR man once said to me "PR everything, and everything's PR-able."
I think the same is true for branding.

It's not an exclusive club, and nor should it be.

So come on all you waste management businesses, chip processors, widget
factories and haulage contractors, where are you?

Just because what you do might appear to be dull to others doesn't mean it is.
Maersk, Blue Circle cement, Chubb, Eddie Stobart, Onyx Waste Management
and thousands of others have all made terrific Brands from apparently very
humdrum activities. There are thousands of Sleeping Beauties out there, as
Robin Wight from WCRS coined them, and I'd love to kiss each and every
one of them.

Sleeping
beauty?

This lesson could also be used for 'tricky' products or services, not just seemingly dull ones.

At the end of 2000 I met David Walter, the then Director of Communications for the Liberal Democrats. We were at a business convention.

Rather like football management, everyone approaches politics with an open mouth and, sadly, I'm no different.

So I set about offering my view on how he and the Party should go about branding themselves and, in a reference to their new leader, asked "and who is this Kennedy anyway?"

David was amazingly patient and unfailingly polite. Once I'd finished my deliverance he pretended to empathise by explaining that part of the Liberal Democrats' problem was that when anyone rang the party out of hours they'd be met with an answerphone message that said "sorry we're not here to take your call. Please leave your message after the high moral tone."

In the course of my enjoying the joke he threw the perfect combination of an upper cut and a judo move on me. "If you really think you can do better perhaps you should come and tell us how."

"Very well," I retorted, "I'd love to," realising that I'd now gone too far to back down from the challenge.

Within a week or so I met Lord Razzall and Lord Rennard for drinks on the terrace at the House of Lords. Tim Razzall had once been European Lawyer of the Year and it showed. He asked piercing questions and displayed the quick mind of an aggressive strategist. Chris Rennard was no walk in the park either. Widely regarded as the country's leading psephologist, he became the Party's CEO and took operational control of all election activities.

I confessed that I hadn't been a committed supporter of the Party but it did at least strike me as being less dogmatic than the others.

"The problem with the others," I offered, "is that they seem to be conditioned to seeing everything either as 'red,' or 'blue.' Whereas I suspect that the British voter is ready for a more sophisticated and, dare I say it, liberal approach."

LIB DEMS TO WIN HERE:

If everyone thinking of voting Lib Dem actually does ...

If you thought that the Liberal Democrats could win in your constituency how would you vote?

Liberal Democrat	39%
Labour	31%
Conservative	26%

Source: Analysis of ICM Poll 17-19th April 2005.

therealalternative.org

LIBERAL DEMOCRATS

They allowed me to carry on. "There are some issues they'd like to be quite blue about and some they'd like to be quite red about. And some, many probably, they'd like in quite a different colour altogether, please. There's your opportunity. Stop thinking of yourselves as the 'third Party,' and start thinking of yourselves as the first Party of fresh thinking."

It seemed to strike a chord, so a meeting with Charles Kennedy was set up. I met him in his flat. He was very relaxed, very polite and, it was obvious from the start, very intelligent. More so than people knew.

I became particularly comfortable when he climbed on to his sofa, kicked off his shoes and lay back, clearly ready for a good long chat. Which is exactly what we did, for four hours, until it was dark outside. Sarah, his then girlfriend and future wife, arrived home to find us lost in our conversation and switched the lights on. So started a long friendship that lasted past two elections.

It wasn't difficult to persuade Charles and the three Lords closest to him, Razzall, Rennard and Newby that it would be good if we could undertake an exercise in 'redefining' the Party for the future. So we gathered the Shadow Cabinet and duly did just that.

I'd not lived through the expression 'herding cats' until that point, and that session gave it new meaning. But they were generous, polite and willing cats throughout.

We concluded that the purpose of a political Party is to define and then plan for the 'ideal' society for its citizens. In their case the style in which they might go about doing that, due in no small part to Charles' manner, would be down to Earth and 'anti-politics,' or what we termed 'real.' So a working notion of

'Real Idealism' was born, to reflect both the ambition of what a Party in power should be about, and the style in which it would conduct itself.

Each of the 'Cabinet Ministers' was given the task of defining what the 'ideal' would be for their Department, based on studying what was considered best in its class from around the world. These findings contributed to the manifesto, and the campaign theme became 'A real chance for real change.'

Over the two elections the results were stunning: in the 2001 election the Party won 52 seats, its highest achievement since 1929. Following this, mid–term, in October '03, YouGov's leadership poll showed Ian Duncan-Smith on an approval rating of 22%, Tony Blair on 40%, and Charles Kennedy on 65%.

In April '05 MORI's poll revealed Kennedy's 'trustworthy' score - an essential part of our 'real' Brand positioning - to be 65% again, with Michael Howard at 36% and Blair on 32%, less than half of Kennedy's score.

In the subsequent election the Party put on a further 10 seats, and was also voted Best Campaign by the British Election Study.

This Brand-centric approach moved Charles to later say that "he has forced me to take a sideways look at politics and the Party's role within it."

For my part, it puts paid to the mistaken view that branding and 'spin' are one and the same.

NOTES

Don't believe that branding is an exclusive club for the rich and beautiful.

A 'yes' answer to these questions means that branding is relevant for you:

1. Do you have customers? YES   NO

2. Do you have competitors? YES   NO

3. Do you have staff? YES   NO

It really is that straightforward.

But the VELUX experience had also taught me a painful lesson.

Whilst a Brand can bring a company and its people along with it, it can only do so at an appropriate pace.

The VELUX campaign was hugely successful at creating interest in the Brand, but we hadn't given enough attention to driving the idea through the business and aligning the organisation to what we were doing.

Amongst other things this had led to problems with supply of the product meeting the demand that was being created. Nice problem to have, some might think, but consumers can be pretty unforgiving when things go wrong in emotive areas like home improvement.

We also launched the TV campaign before linking the idea through all the other communications channels and, crucially, the staff.

Schoolboy errors, all of them, but they were inexperienced and we were young.

It brought me to rule eight:

rule 8

Don't let your Brand run too far ahead of your business.

While a company's Brand should always be inspirational and aspirational the skill lies in knowing how far to pitch it. Too low and it's not ambitious or motivational enough; too high and it becomes make-believe, a fertile breeding ground for the cynics and nay-sayers.

But the last word on this needs to go to Michael Rasmussen, our enthusiastic, young and bright day-to-day Client at VELUX. In the course of a conversation about how things were going so well in one way and yet not so well in another, he said in his perfect but heavily accented English, "Robert, you know the expression 'having your feet on the ground'?"

"Of course, Michael. I do," I replied.

"Well," he continued, "ours are several feet under it."

It was his way of telling me we were running too far ahead of where they were.

NOTES

Don't let your Brand run too far ahead of your business.

1. Does the way you promote the Company feel like it's 'not us'?

2. Is your product or service capable of delivering against the promises being made, whether actual or inferred?

3. Is internal repair needed before you can put a spotlight on the organisation? If so, where?

Chapter 9
1996; haircare, make-up and principles

Before starting the business I had heard the expression 'the only ship you should never set sail in is a partnership.'

In '96 the good ship Bean MC hit a rock. It wouldn't be the last time I'd encounter such problems.

Despite the terrific financial success of the business we had problems among the partners. I wanted to go more up-stream, others wanted to stay put. So this led to a change in line-up and name, with two of the partners leaving.

BANC was formed. It was an attempt to broaden the Company's offering into more Brand-related services.

One of our first opportunities in this new guise was to advise The Body Shop on how to sharpen up their Brand and to help structure their UK communications. It was the first time they had sought external advice of this sort.

I became very excited at the prospect of helping to re-kindle such a big and famous household name. It was only 20 years old but it was already a worldwide phenomenon.

So I read every word about them, in every book, every article and on every scrap of paper that we could get our hands on. I went on the factory tour – twice. I spoke to everyone and anyone – product managers, shop staff, factory workers, receptionists, customers, ex-customers, friends and foes of the Company - anyone who could offer any kind of insight into what made The Body Shop tick.

It was obvious at all levels that the people at The Body Shop had a tremendous belief in what they did, and they had real attitude – in the best possible way. But, nobody, not even founder Anita Roddick, could agree on the articulation of what The Body Shop Brand really stood for.

I'd had more than 100 responses to the question, but no real answers.

She, of course, took a particular pleasure in hearing this, describing the result as 'unsurprising' given that she had so long encouraged 'originality' and 'individuality.' Nevertheless she could see the point I was getting at and applied all her not inconsiderable energy to the challenge.

Anita was a bundle of energy, busy-bodying herself in a hundred things at once and yet somehow staying focused on her bigger aims. She might easily have been the inventor of the phrase 'multi-tasking,' and, if not, it was surely created with her in mind.

Whilst she was famous for campaigning, her greatest and least celebrated strength was her creativity. She had a genuine appreciation and understanding of how to make ideas come to life in innovative, striking, often controversial ways. It was all part of her quest to shake up the Establishment and do things differently. She was extremely comfortable with words and pictures and, in another life, could easily have been a Creative Director of any of the ad agencies I'd worked at.

Perhaps more surprising was that, despite her strident campaigning stances, she was actually confrontation-averse, preferring to find 'alternative' solutions to suggestions that she didn't like, rather than simply turning them down flat. There was a price to pay for this, as anyone who worked there knew.

I liked her and her warmth enormously but she rarely sat still for long enough for there to be much debate about things.

One afternoon, in what must have been our 11th meeting on the subject, one of The Body Shop marketing people mumbled, "Well, we do have this thing we've been wondering about that we call 'well-being.'"

Eureka! I leapt up from the table, hugged her and virtually lifted her off the floor. She seemed visibly shocked by this display of affection but I knew it was a big moment. I thanked her for being a genius and excused myself from the meeting, so I could rush off and get on with it.

"Well-being."
Eureka!

One of the results was the production of a hand-made paper book, called 'The Body Shop; a Source of Well-Being.'

The book became our bible.

'Well being' worked so well because it unified The Body Shop's principles and its products around a single thought. It was soon developed to become 'Principled Well-Being,' to make it more ownable, and to reflect their commitment to the principles they were founded on and by which they lived.

It also helped them make strategic decisions with more consistency and purpose. An early example of this was a decision to launch an aromatherapy range instead of a Tangerine Bubble Bath product. Not a difficult one perhaps – it delivered more well-being and was more 'principled' – but before 'principled well-being' they both had an equal footing in the new product development budget. The previous biggest criterion for selecting which range to develop – after the financials, rightly – would have been 'he who shouted loudest.'

'Principled well-being' was another great example of providing a company with 'a vision of the cathedral whilst they mixed the cement.' It helped throughout the organisation, including in-store, where they focused harder on how to provide 'well-being' for customers. Suddenly smells and sounds became important commercial, retail and Brand considerations.

The Body Shop helped me to learn another important lesson:

rule 9

Keep searching to find your truth; it'll liberate you and your people.

The patience and insistence of finding Anita's 'truth' was paying off, with the army of franchisees telling me that this work had, at last, made more sense of their roles in the organisation than anything like it had done before.

They said they had a new understanding of the Company and, armed with the knowledge that it came from the 'truth' of the place, they felt empowered to take decisions on its behalf as long as they stayed faithful to the idea.

Anita's vision of growing a powerful Brand whilst encouraging freedom and 'individuality' within the business had been given a helping hand.

This lesson bore fruit years later when I landed the contract with Honda, to help them rediscover their 'truth.'

I had been briefed by Ken Keir, the UK Managing Director and VP Europe, to recapture the essence of Soichiro Honda, who had died eight years previously. Ken's concern was that with every passing year the essence of the Honda culture would become dissipated unless it was defined and expressed. He wanted me to search the company until we found and articulated Soichiro's 'truth.'

Ken was the kind of man my friend Stephen Goodyear, the CEO of
Young & Co, brewers of the famous Youngs Bitter and owners of London's
best pub estate, would describe as the sort who 'doesn't disappoint.' Steady,
unscrupulously honest, thoughtful and deeply dependable.

He assigned Simon Thompson to the task. Simon was Honda's man responsible
for Special Projects at the time. It was obvious from the moment we met that
he was an extraordinary character. I've always believed it's better to tame a wild
horse than flog a dead one, and if ever there was a perfect example of a wild
horse it was Simon. He was as wild as they come.

"OK," he started. "Forget everything you thought you knew about this
company and everything you've heard. I'm also not going to let you to speak
to the dealers, journalists and all the other people that you'll want to speak to
because the real brief is this: we're seen as sensible, but dull. We don't mind
the sensible bit, but dull we ain't. Can you fix it?"

It was a clear brief.

It meant spending a lot of time with him and Ken getting to the bottom of
'Honda-ness.' Again, I read the books and, again, I tried to absorb everything
and anything that I could.

It quickly became clear that Honda's passion was motorbikes. It's where it all
started for them but, more telling than that, it was where they really came alive.

Nowhere more so than at the TT races on the Isle of Man.

Simon and I flew out there early one morning where I met the Honda Team –
the riders, their concerned families, the mechanics who the riders relied on to
keep them alive, and the support staff. They were hard-core, grease under the
fingernails bikers, every one of them. The atmosphere was a strange brew of
tension, excitement and real fear. Above all, it was deadly serious. But I hadn't
seen anything yet.

I was taken to a corner on the circuit at the base of a long downhill stretch.
We stood there looking high up to our right waiting for the first of the riders to
appear. A few minutes later two did, breaking the horizon line as their black,
silhouetted figures stood out against the slate grey sky. Within fractions of

seconds they screamed down the hill past us throwing a sharp right at the last moment to climb the next stretch to our left, away from our sights. It was a blur and we were left with the tangy smell of petrol, oil and hot rubber. More riders appeared, this time in clumps of three or four, jockeying for position as they flung themselves into the treacherous bend.

It was the curb-side that scared me most. One nudge of that and it would be certain death for any of them. They were missing it by inches, trying to reduce it to millimetres. And they kept coming, wave after wave of them.

It was becoming obvious to me... dull they ain't.

After many stories about Mr Honda's vision, about how they decided not only to get into Formula 1 but to win it within a certain time limit, their pioneering work with robots, the amazing tales of how the motorbike racing started and continued, and the fact that, at only 52 years old, they were the world's biggest producers of engines, I concluded that ordinary words couldn't describe this extraordinary company. I had no option but to invent a new one for them.

The day of the meeting with Ken and Simon arrived. I was due to report back my findings for what had been the most idiosyncratic of briefings. I explained that they struck me as being part-visionaries and part-engineers. This combination led to an ugly word but one that they agreed captured them perfectly: 'Visioneers' – a group of people engaged in 'visioneering,' whose ambitious visions were matched by their engineering capability to fulfill them.

There was no doubt this was their 'truth,' even if the route we took to find it was unconventional.

"It's true," said Ken. "That's exactly what we are."

Simon was less demure...

"That's cock-on"

... he asserted, with some excitement. It's an expression I hadn't heard before nor, oddly, since.

"But what kind of visioneering do we do?" he asked. It was a typically intense Simon question. Warming to his theme he pressed on. "If 'visioneering' is what we do, how do we go about doing it?"

It caused me to withdraw and have a think. On returning a few days later I explained that the outstanding feature of 'Honda-ness' within 'visioneering' was their sheer will to make things happen. It was a determination that knew no bounds. I wanted to call it 'indomitable' but we all agreed that wouldn't travel well. It was Mr Honda's irrepressible spirit that made them the way they are so it was agreed that they were 'spirited visioneers.'

It was sent to Japan for approval. They had been working on the same problem and had arrived at a similar point. Their iteration of it was the now famous 'The Power of Dreams.'

I argued that to be strictly faithful to the idea I might have expressed it as 'Powered *by* Dreams,' but they were having none of it so I backed off on the grounds that it was their Brand not mine.

Ken told me a story a long while later about this work. "It sits on my desk every day," he said. "Last week they sent me a new recruit for our post room to look over before we hired him. I thought to myself "Does he have a vision for how he's going to execute his work? Does he have the 'engineering' ability to fulfil that vision? Does he have the right Honda 'spirit'?" When I decided that the answer to all three was 'yes,' we took him on.

With him also saying "we use this work as the business driver that determines the future of the Honda Brand," this golden rule clearly struck a chord with him.

NOTES

Keep searching to find your truth; it'll liberate you and your people.

1. Has a proper study been conducted into determining your 'truth' – or values, or has someone just alighted on a set of words that are hard to disagree with? (Be honest...)

2. Are your findings a) meaningful, b) motivating and, above all c) true to you?

3. Do you accept that fully understanding your 'truth' is an ongoing search, or do you feel that, once articulated, the job's done?

In slightly different 'truth-searching' exercises for Metro and The Evening Standard, Mike Anderson, now Managing Director of The Sun and News of the World, was also struck by this rule.

We worked together when he was MD of both titles. Mike is a burly Scot whose two outstanding features beyond his sheer physicality are his instinct and his courage.

He's definitely another wild horse.

I've lost count of the number of times I've taken a call from him saying "I've had an idea in the shower…" These shower moments either made my blood run cold, requiring me to work hard at carefully talking him off the ledge, or they were the rays of sunshine that made life more joyous. There wasn't much in between.

I was in the shower this morning and thought wouldn't it be a good idea if…

You're not going to like this but…

What do you think about this…

I had this great idea…

I was thinking about that chat we had yesterday…

Do you think we should do something more radical…

In our conversations it quickly became clear that newspapers were no longer really in the business of breaking news. That position had been stolen by the broadcast media and, in particular, the internet. It was an alarming discovery.

The Evening Standard's 'truth' was that it was a companion for London travellers, there, as we called it, 'to stimulate their enquiring minds.'

This realisation led to a cessation of the expensive editions structure they had had for years, where they published five different editions a day, with all the attendant distribution costs, in an attempt to keep up in the un-winnable race of 'breaking news.'

'Stimulating enquiring minds' didn't need five editions a day. 'Breaking news' might have done, but the model no longer worked.

Mike cut it to three, and introduced 'Lite,' – one of the more joyous shower moments – a radical free evening paper. It pre-empted the imminent arrival of News International's The London Paper and it protected Associated's position in the sector.

Part of what gave him the confidence to play such radical strokes was that he knew he was armed with the Brand's 'truth.'

Metro's 'truth' was that it delivered a previously untapped audience, dubbed 'urbanites.' These were young, professional people who had fallen out of the newspaper reading market but who would be happy to read a free morning news digest that was presented in a punchy, apolitical and unpretentious way.

They had an urbanite attitude – as opposed to a suburbanite one – and worked in the city even if they didn't live there.

In its early days Metro didn't have a tremendously powerful set of numbers to boast about to advertisers. But Mike always knew that its 'truth,' the fact that it uniquely spoke to a very valuable group of new readers, was an important asset. To that end, he charged a rate for space in the paper that was out of all proportion to the conventions of the industry, sold it hard, and stood by his conviction.

And they came, in their droves, and paid up.

We became firm friends and he always told me that the mantra 'keep searching for your truth' has provided him with "the best business lesson I've ever had."

He is a bear of a man, and it was little surprise when Rupert Murdoch hired him into News International's stable where he continues to frighten and delight colleagues and associates in equal measure.

We've covered nine golden rules. So what's the half? The half isn't a half because it's smaller. It's a half because no matter how far I go I don't think it's a subject that will ever be completed.

I make little apology for how obvious and simple this one is.

In American English, 'It's about the people, stoopid.'

Successful branding only works with focused and motivated people. Whether they're in the factory, the call-centre, or out on the road selling things, how they deliver the quality, value and promise of a Brand is critical to its success. How they do it internally with their colleagues, with the trade, with suppliers, with customers, with everyone who touches it – simply can't be overlooked.

This is becoming more and more important in a service-based economy. Product parity is now easier than ever to achieve and the consumer's voice, amplified by near endless word of mouth digital communications channels, can make or break businesses easier than ever before.

Which organisations are people going to be drawn to in the future, whether customers, consumers or employees? Organisations with strong, well-defined and consistent Brands, run by and represented by people who are clear about their purpose and believe in what they're doing.

Just pay a visit to the Apple store or Innocent's HQ at 'Fruit Towers' to see this in action. They're in another dimension.

The days of hiding behind a product, no matter how good it might be, are over. People nowadays want to know who and what's behind a Brand and, alongside the quality of the product or service, they'll accept or reject that Brand based on its values. And when the Brand and the business name are the same – and most are – that has big implications on how the business treats and trains its people in the understanding of what their Brand is all about.

'Engaging your people is becoming more and more important in a service-based economy.'

So, golden rule 91/2 is…

Your Brand needs to be strong on the inside before it can ever be strong on the outside.

What reaches the outside always starts on the inside. So if it's no good there it won't be any good later.

That's also why 'branding' can't just be a corporate identity makeover which, for many companies, is about as effective as applying lipstick to a pig.

Eugene Hughes, the founder of an excellent Company called People Brands, complains that "businesses can be such toxic places." He sees his mission in life as changing this.

For my part, engaging them with a meaningful focus like the definition of what their Brand stands for is a great start to the detox process.

Smart companies, First Direct and lastminute.com among them, are increasingly focused on employing and training people who can deliver their service in the Brand's unique way.

But some are even more dedicated.

Zeev Godik (pronounced 'Zevi') founder and CEO of the hugely successful and fast-growing Gaucho Restaurants empire, puts new managers through a 3-month training programme before they ever set foot in the restaurant they're going to manage.

Three months... On full pay...

He says it's the most important and best investment he makes, adding that "Brand standards transcend personal ones. Brand standards and Brand practices are non-negotiable. Second best, either in action or attitude, is not an option."

If a principle isn't a principle until it costs you money, then training his people around 'Brand standards' is a pretty important principle for Zeev.

No wonder it's such a success.

The simple fact is that it takes a lot more than the usual lip service that most companies give it.

Too many HR Directors don't seem to grasp this, and it continues to baffle me why. If they struggle with credibility in the Boardroom, as so many Marketing Directors do, they could do themselves a big favour by taking the mantle for driving and maintaining the 'Brand standards' through each and every individual in the business. Recruitment, induction, training, learning and development, appraisals, incentives, bonuses and staff surveys are all important opportunities to reinforce the Brand message and create consistency.

And the same could be true for Marketing people, if they were to reflect more faithfully the same Brand thinking in new product or service development and all the organisation's internal and external communications.

HR and Marketing working together on this, under the CEO's auspices, is an all too rare but devastatingly powerful combination. The right people, pointing in the same direction, will end up delivering the right product and creating the right reputation.

NOTES

Your Brand needs to be strong on the inside before it can ever be strong on the outside.

1. How aligned is your organisation, at Board level, the leadership team, and below?

2. How vibrant is the internal Culture? Is it measured? Against what criteria?

3. How clearly and consistently is your Brand reflected in everything the organisation does internally, from recruitment to induction to incentives packages?

Chapter 10
Adding it all up

'In short, the future means
no Brand, no business.'

To round off the golden rules rule it's worth summarising the 'Know Thyself' trail we've taken:

Birdseye's pre-emptive attack on private label taught me that…

1. Your Brand isn't an optional extra; it's a genuinely powerful competitive weapon.

These days this is more true than ever.

In consumer or business-to-business markets, or in charities, NGOs, political parties, universities, art galleries and even countries, Brands and branding are here to stay. The Guggenheim or The Tate are Brands, Becks, Posh and Jordan are Brands, Oxfam, The Red Cross and the UN are Brands, Germany, Japan, Morocco, Jamaica and hundreds of other countries are Brands. (We know that England is confused about its…)

More recently, we've had the Archbishop of Canterbury referring to the Virgin Mary as "a global Brand," erudite debates on Radio 4 as to whether Handel or Bach was the bigger Brand, and even the Camell Laird shipyard being bought because "Cammell Laird is an internationally recognized Brand which carries tremendous goodwill when bidding for contracts."

They all use their Brand – according to their skill at implementing it, as competitive weapons that differentiate them in their own unique ways.

In short, the future means no Brand, no business.

Hail Mary

Rowan Williams on how the mother of Jesus became a global brand

...ll it the ultimate theo-
...to-riches story: how a
insignificant   young
...m a backwater of the
...pire became one of the
...instantly recognisable
the world. Exactly how
...inating story. Some-

Heinz, Homebase and VAX taught me...

2. Get the proposition right.
It probably isn't what you think it is.

Not all that glitters about a product or service is its most golden proposition.
Sometimes it's a product claim and sometimes it's an ownable customer
insight. The most powerful propositions are usually a truthful and meaningful
combination of both.

With Vauxhall, I learned...

3. The company structure shouldn't define your Brand;
your Brand should define the company structure.

How people buy cars became more important than how Vauxhall made them.

Lawrie Haynes, Richard Branson, and other enlightened CEOs and their
advisers, are increasingly taking the view that, beyond structural issues, the
branding consideration in the mergers and acquisitions process is fundamental
for future success.

It's widely accepted that more than 50% of mergers and acquisitions fail due to
a lack of 'culture fit.' Thereby arguing that culture fit is every bit as important as
structure fit.

From the Masters of Brand management, BMW, I learned...

4. Branding is about winning in your own way.

It's the bottom line for what branding is really about, and Tom Purves' words
ring in my ears every day.

As do the expansive thoughts of Norman Strauss and BT…

5. All good communication is based on reciprocating confidences.

If it doesn't move people in some way then it's just wasting your money.

But BT taught me more than one lesson. This second one is no less important…

6. Great Brands need great humans to champion them.

If it weren't for Adrian Hosford, much of BT's change would never have happened. Great champions are an under-acknowledged species, and deserve identifying, promoting and protecting for lasting Brand success.

VELUX windows taught me that there are no boring products…

7. Branding is not an exclusive club for the rich and beautiful.

Even seemingly dull products can be powerfully branded. Whether it's business-to-business, business-to-consumer, or other, 'everything and anything's brand-able.'

VELUX also taught me the painful, but crucial lesson that…

8. A Brand can't run too far ahead of its company.

The Brand can and should be aspirational, and inspire everyone in the company to reach higher and farther – but it can't be out of reach.

The Body Shop and Honda solidified something that I knew instinctively, and is in fact the thing that gets me out of bed each morning…

9. Keep searching until you find your truth.

Every Brand really does have one.

9 ½. Your Brand needs to be strong on the inside before it can ever be strong on the outside.

Whilst the external projection is critical, if it isn't aligned with internal beliefs and behaviours people will see through it and it won't be sustainable.

'The simple truth is that Brands are inside-out creatures.'

NOTES

The nine and a half rules.

1. How many of these rules does your organisation currently subscribe to?

2. If it has missed some, could that provide a clue as to what might be going wrong?

3. Are there other rules of your own that, added to these, would enhance your organisation's performance?

Chapter 11
The principle of the Single Organising Principle

In 2003 I realised that I had been falling steadily out of love with the business I'd founded.

I wanted to have a company that devoted itself completely to consulting for organisations at the highest strategic level, focused on helping them develop their most potent under-exploited asset, their Brand.

BANC wasn't that Company.

So I sold it. But not before making a few discoveries that were to have a deep and lasting impact on me.

It's fair to say that in the latter years of BANC's life I had taken my eye of the financial ball. The company had always done well. We had had an extremely happy ship, a steady stream of new business and plenty of good media coverage.

But, as it turned out, we were living well beyond our means and, when a major Client took their work in-house as a cost-saving measure, the cashflow dried up.

And so did we.

I learnt, the hard way, that John Bartle (co-founder of Bartle Bogle Hegarty) was right when he said 'Profile is vanity; profit is sanity.'

It became a fire-sale, to a new AIM-listed plc in the sector called Media Square. On the surface of things it seemed like a mutually workable strategic fit, but culturally it proved to be a disaster (surprise, surprise...).

Media Square shut the limited company down, and although I now found myself as Chairman of the BANC Group of Companies, which included their PR and Design businesses, it wasn't the company I'd wanted it to become.

And I was a long way from pursuing my dream.

The whole process of closing down a business was grisly beyond compare. Although we managed to avoid more job losses, there was the daily stench of failure, shame, and guilt, leave aside the dreadful anxiety of wondering how things were going to work out in the future.

Put simply, it was the most humiliating and frightening period of my life, during which I saw the worst side of a number of people.

To the extent I hadn't previously believed possible.

I wouldn't wish the experience on anyone but, as with all clouds, it did bring a silver lining. And that was my new appreciation of the simple but important nuts and bolts of running a business.

Beyond overheads, cashflow and margins, the fiduciary minutiae of running a business took on a new significance for me. These learnings are now essential ingredients in not only how I run my own business, but also in how I assess my Clients' businesses.

Despite helping put two of my children through private schooling, as well as employing more than 50 people in its time, I still considered BANC to be a failure. But I became comforted about this by Henry Ford, no less, when I discovered his visionary declaration that "failure is simply the opportunity to begin again, this time more intelligently."

"Failure is simply the opportunity to begin again, this time more intelligently."

So I did.

I saw that there was room in the market for a new kind of Management Consultancy, one whose start-point was Brand development. After all, the accounting boys had managed to get themselves taken seriously at the strategic level, as had the IT boys, the logistics boys and even the engineers. The summit was under assault from all comers but, with only one or two notable exceptions, next to nobody from the branding world was carrying a flag.

By now Brands and branding were well established on the business agenda, if little understood and little practiced.

I called it Northstar.

The North star is the only one in the constellation that's in a fixed position. Once you find it the rest of the world starts to fall into place.

Northstar took these rules and my career's worth of learnings, and condensed them into a model that is now the basis of the business' modus operandi.

The lessons from these great companies and the people who had been around to teach me made me draw a few simple but very powerful conclusions.

The first was that success was never down to one individual. Yes, he or she can be the visionary, the inspiration, the keeper of the faith and the enforcer, but real success only ever came when a group of people were motivated to work together towards one goal.

That made me realise the importance and value of creating and fostering a culture.

The second was the continuous reiteration of the fact that 'even the most powerful Brand in the world has an outstanding product at its heart.' Every one of the companies I worked with had done the hard bit: they'd invested in creating an outstanding product or service. They were now looking to capitalise on their investment by transforming their offerings from products into Brands.

Skoda, one of the great Brand turnarounds of our times, simply wouldn't have happened without radical product improvement. First Direct could never have succeeded just because it was a new and different kind of bank. It was the service that made the difference.

Thirdly, it seemed that without creating and managing the right reputation – mostly through the use of good communications – it was very hard for these organisations to draw attention to their great products either from customers or potential staff.

The Single Organising Principle, and more.

So the first premise of the Northstar model is that businesses can be broken down into three distinct areas: their Culture, their Product or Service, and their Reputation. (See fig 1)

The Culture of an organisation drives everything else.

I think of this as 'what we value around here.' The people we hire, what we celebrate, what we frown upon, even how we are about money – borrowers or lenders, short-term or long.

Rousseau's advice to 'look to the origin' is crucial here, in understanding the true tendency of a business. Time and time again I've found that the original DNA of a business will still be present years later, even if the organisation has undergone many different periods of leadership and, often, ownership.

Start-up principles change but they're amazingly durable. It's uncanny how their integrity survives.

Great products and great reputations can be driven into the ground by lousy cultures, and it's leadership that drives Culture. That's why Culture starts and stops with the CEO and his or her team. They are the ones responsible for enforcing the values and creating a climate of understanding, stability and consistency around the place.

The Product or Service is the front-line soldier for the business. It's what the enterprise does. It's the bit the consumer or customer interacts with. It's the thing that keeps people coming back for more, time after time – or not.

Whilst it needs a Reputation to get people to come to it in the first place, and it's reliant on a Culture that nurtures and cares for it, it's obviously pretty damned important in its own right, otherwise a business has no tomorrow.

And Reputation, heavily influenced by communications, is the vehicle that delivers customers and future employees – profitably. It sets up the promises for the Product to deliver against repeatedly.

That one-two combination – 'Promises Delivered,' if you like – is what creates consistency. Which, in turn, breeds Trust. Once you've gained your customer's Trust, they'll cross the street to buy from you over your rival. Not only does that help with valuable lower cost repeat purchasers, it also allows you to charge a reasonable premium.

At its simplest, these three areas are the ones that govern organisations, irrespective of size or sector.

fig 1

But, beyond this, and beyond understanding each of these in turn, the first and most fundamental step is to find the binding agent that aligns them together.

This is the Single Organising Principle. (See fig 2)

It's called the Single Organising Principle because:

a) it must be single-minded so as to remove any opportunity for unfocused, fuzzy or lazy thinking

b) it must come from the principles of the business, and be their 'Truth,' not just be idealised thinking that is just grafted on

c) it must be a principle that helps people inside the business organise themselves by making clear, consistent and confident decisions. It's not just a list of 'rules & regs,' it's a motivating mechanic intended to provide people with what John King, CEO of House of Fraser calls "Freedom within a Framework."

"Freedom within a Framework."

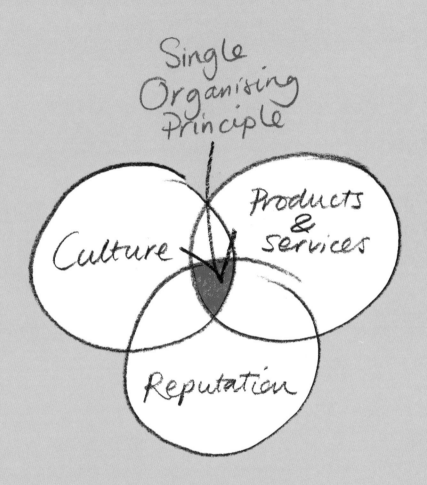

fig 2

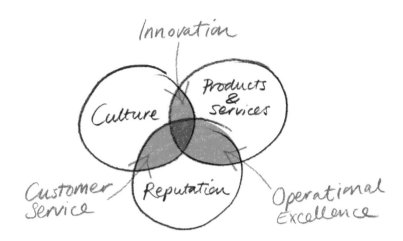

fig 2a

Relevant innovation is the result of a company's Culture and Product/Service portfolio being brought together in light of the Single Organising Principle.

Appropriate customer service is delivered when a company's Culture and Reputation are driven by the Single Organising Principle.

And consistent operational excellence informed by the Single Organising Principle means that a company's Products and Services will enhance its Reputation. And vice versa. (See fig 2a)

The truth of this approach is that any organisation which succeeds in aligning itself consistently over time will be more financially aerodynamic than one that doesn't.

Good examples of this are Channel 4, Innocent, Apple, BMW and others. These companies are seamlessly aligned, where you can't put a 'fag-paper' between their Culture, their Product and their Reputation. (See fig 3.) Customers know exactly what they're going to get from them, and they deliver against their promise over and over again.

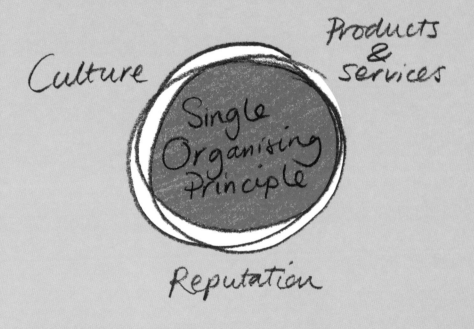

Culture

Products & services

Single Organising Principle

Reputation

fig 3

These beacon Brands exist in every sector but sadly, many of them are woefully under-exploited or, worse, seemingly unaware of it.

An equally compelling argument for taking this approach is the financial one, which can be argued with a simple logic:

– Alignment around a Single Organising Principle = efficiencies. Because everyone's pulling in the same direction you can either do more for the same cost, or achieve the same for less. Either way, you're being more efficient.

– As such it makes you more profitable, (NOTE: efficiencies don't guarantee you profit – that's down to you. But they do allow you to be more profitable.)

– It follows then that alignment = profitability.

Over time, consistent alignment will lead to sustainable profitability, one of the key determinants of shareholder value.

So, in conclusion, aside from creating clear differentiation and providing everyone involved with a clear sense of purpose, Brands add value.

Or, in plain Northern English, Brands = brass.

Alignment = Efficiencies = Profitability

Consistent Alignment = Sustainable Profitability

= Shareholder Value

=

Irrespective of where a conversation with a Client starts, as was the case with Iain Ferguson, Tate & Lyle's visionary and highly personable CEO's plea of "I just want us to all speak with one instinct," (we both knew exactly what he meant…) or another Client whose complaint was "we can't get products to market fast enough," or another in the service sector's "the competition are wiping out any differentiation we have," or even simply, and commonly, "we don't think our communications are working hard enough," I argue that all these issues are inter-related within the three areas of Culture, Product/Service, and Reputation.

They're all linked to each other, and to look at them in isolation is to miss the point.

That's the beauty of Brands and the Branding process. It no more sits in the Marketing Department than it does in HR, Commercial, Legal, Operations, Finance, Business Development, Communications, Sales or any other department that I might have left out here. In other words…
it's only everywhere.

That's why it's so important.

That's why smart CEOs need to treasure, grow, nurture, stroke, stretch, push, pull, promote, protect, care about, worry about and, above all, look after their Brand.

Properly.

If they do, it'll look after them.

And their people.

NOTES

The single organising principle.

1. What is your 'strongest suit?' Your Culture, your Product/Service, or your Reputation?

2. If you were to score each of them out of 10, how wide would the disparity between the 'best' and the 'worst' be?

3. In thinking about fixing the misalignment between any two or all three, is it clear how the other two or three areas would be instrumental in creating alignment? If so, who would need to be involved in the conversations?

'The Brand definition, like a Constitution, is based on fundamental principles; it is therefore a truly democratic piece of intellectual capital, created from the views of many, made on behalf of all.'

A paradox of the Single Organising Principle is that it is one thought, arrived at by many.

The very basis on which it succeeds is that it is a collective discovery, not the view solely of the CEO, or the Board, or the external consultants, or the Chairman's PA. As Dr Nick Georgiades put it: "People support that which they help create." It's human nature.

So at the heart of arriving at the Single Organising Principle is a two-day workshop, attended by a dozen or so people from across the organisation. When bullied in the past we've managed it in a day and a half, but I prefer it over two days. It allows for ideas to be aired and discussed rather than just a slavish following of the process with one anxious eye on the clock.

After all, we're only building the foundations of our future…

A vitally important moment in the proceedings has next to nothing to do with the workshop itself; it's the dinner that breaks up the two days. It never ceases to amaze me how little companies do this sort of thing, and sometimes listening to very senior people discussing things over dinner in a way that they obviously never have before is a sweet & sour experience. Sweet because it's evident they're really getting value out of it, but slightly sour at the surprise that they haven't done it before. Leave aside often.

Perhaps that's why 'It's good to Talk' worked so well. It just is.

Casting for the workshop is crucial. The most important criterion for the list of attendees is breadth. It needs the widest gamut of representation possible, to make sure that whatever conclusions are reached are not overly influenced by any one interested party.

The Brand definition, like a Constitution, is based on fundamental principles. It is therefore a truly democratic piece of intellectual capital, created from the views of many, made on behalf of all.

As such, it demands that all walks of the organisation's life contribute fully to its formation.

More often than not this means that the senior team, or the 'Leadership team,' are the chosen ones. It's certainly helpful to have representatives with weight in the organisation, as the real work starts after the workshop when the Principle needs campaigning internally.

But a willing heart is always better than a heavyweight heart.

In terms of set-up, it's much better to run workshops off-site. It adds to the drama, and is a potent signal from the organisation to the delegates that, in Johnny Rotten's immortal words, "we mean it, man."

Psychologically people are also more prepared to abandon their mobile phones for a few hours which, coupled with the fact that they won't be dressed in 'office gear,' makes them all the more able to respond to the stimulus of the session as humans rather than titles.

'A willing heart is better than a heavyweight heart.'

The session itself covers seven areas:

1. Who is your 'sweet-spot' target audience?

Every organisation has a multitude of audiences it needs to address.
But few really do the work to dig a bit deeper and ask themselves
who, fundamentally, is their key target audience.

I had the unusual privilege recently to work with a start-up plc in the
pharmaceuticals sector. This particular question was put to the CEO, Robert
Mansfield, a man as charismatic as he is thoughtful. It was put as "Robert,
who is this Company really for?" He had been told he wasn't allowed to say
"shareholders," and "staff," as they are givens.

Whilst there was plenty of debate around the subject, it was relatively
straightforward for a start-up to be clear about who it was really in
business to serve.

But for more mature organisations, especially those whose market-places are
changing, this can be a complex question and one that they often shy away
from addressing in an attempt to keep their appeal 'broad.' Nothing wrong
with wanting that, but it does need to be based on an understanding on
who, above all others, is the primary group.

This is so that future Brand strategies can be made with the confidence that
the organisation's greatest supporters will be willing to follow.

In super-complex situations, where advanced market segmentation studies are
called for, an under-utilised tool for identifying linkages between what might
appear to be equally important groups is the use of psychographics. This goes
beyond mere demographics, and defines people by their attitudes to sectors,
products, or life. It's a subject for a whole separate book, but it's useful at
drawing pen portraits of different groups.

Generally, consumer and Media companies are information-rich but
insight-poor. And business-to-business companies often know their
customers by name, but equally don't know much about them.

That's why there's a gaping opportunity for it to be done differently and better.

2. What are their motivations?

When IBM ran advertising that said 'Nobody got fired for buying IBM,' they evidently knew that they were selling more than mainframe computers. They understood that for the person buying the computers – or recommending them to their Boards – there was a lot of money at stake and with that, their job.

What a great insight. How reassuring for any potential buyer. What a pity the rest of the Company couldn't keep up with the ingenuity of this insight...

This question in the session is designed to flush out what is the real human substance the organisation is dealing with. What are the deeper motives behind people's interest in the category they're trading in? Is insurance really about reassurance? As we saw earlier, is the real motivation behind vacuum cleaning really about 'visibly clean,' rather than 'deep clean?' Are GPs really seeking 'efficacy' out of the goodness of their hearts when they prescribe, or is it because they really don't want serially ill people cluttering up their surgeries?

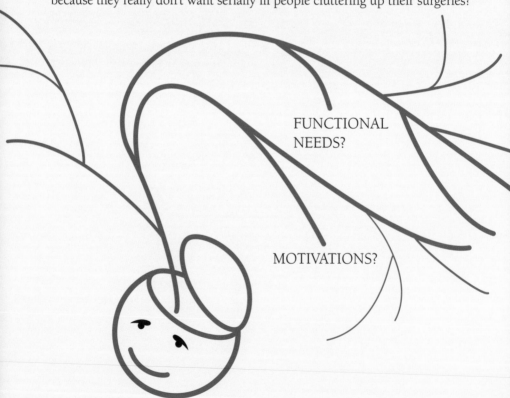

FUNCTIONAL
NEEDS?

MOTIVATIONS?

In business-to-business cases it tends to be more rational, but there are often deeper motives than the ones that present themselves. Why does 'on-time delivery' really matter? Or 'after sales customer care'? Why is 'choice of supplier' so important for some companies? Understanding these more profound motivations can start to affect how your Brand presents itself and its products and services to its audiences.

This work can be done in a separate research programme where it can be gone into in more depth, but it's better if it can also be covered in the session itself, alongside research findings. That way everyone contributes again, and they can see the workings out in the margins.

In the course of investigating motivations, often using mind-maps, hundreds of possible motivations are dug up. 99.9 percent of them will be discarded when the team is then asked to choose which ones they think the Company is capable of commandeering as their own.

Or, put more poetically, 'which river we think we can ride.'

This can produce a shortlist of up to 10 or so, but it's better to condense it down to four or five, which they will be asked to shorten even further a little later on.

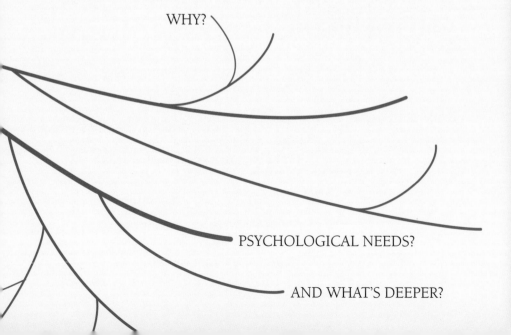

WHY?

PSYCHOLOGICAL NEEDS?

AND WHAT'S DEEPER?

3. How are you different from, or better than, your competitors?

Delegates will have been asked to team up and come prepared with a short, punchy presentation extolling the virtues of a competitor they've been asked to represent. Four or five competitors will do.

Roughly 10 bullet points are all that's needed, but they should to be factual, as detailed as possible, and designed to hurt.

The simple definition of a competitor is anyone who could lay claim to the same pound, dollar or Euro that you're chasing. But sometimes it's less obvious.

Isn't 'going to the pub' a possible competitor for a television channel? In b2b, couldn't the customer's own internal service provider be a competitor?

'A competitor is anyone who could lay claim to the same pound, dollar or Euro that you're chasing.'

These lateral thoughts are often missed and, with them, so too are opportunities.

In their teams, the delegates are asked to make their 'pitches,' trying to persuade the rest of the group about the unique strengths of the organisation they're representing. There are the inevitable howls of protest from the faithful others but the presenters should be allowed to finish their turn before the group responds.

A good moderator will listen out for the sounds of a barrel being scraped and call a close to proceedings before anyone gets hurt…

Some of these pitches can be so good that members of the group can end up with their head in their hands, wondering if they can join the Company they've just been hearing about. But that, believe it or not, is a good sign. If your muscles don't ache a bit when you're exercising then you're probably not trying hard enough.

Once each presentation is finished, the group fights back. When doing so, they're only allowed to talk about themselves, and not to rubbish the competition. That's much too easy.

The opposition's points are taken and either bettered by the Home Team, or quietly conceded whilst other points of difference are sought.

Once this process has been gone through for the four or five competitors, a small number of points will have emerged as ones that the team will have consistently relied on to beat off each and all of the competitors.

These are recorded as our proprietary and sustainable differences.

4. Purpose statement

Having identified the primary target audience, mined for their motivations, and uncovered our competitive differences, it's time to combine these findings together into a single compelling statement. This will define our Purpose, as it fuses the most powerful customer motivation with the most powerful competitive difference.

This means that we're articulating a Purpose that:
a) has meaning amongst customers, and
b) is exclusive to us.

Delegates are each asked to write their version of the statement and share it with the group until there is agreement around one definitive statement.

No-one leaves the room until there's agreement.

I've known it take 26 drafts before there was a happy consensus, but it's worth the pain. It's a pivotal moment in shaping the overall Brand proposition.

5. Values and Personality

The Purpose statement is a 'bald' statement laying out the shape of the Brand's future footprint. The values ground it and the Personality adds colour and texture.

The delegates are asked to select imagery that they believe represents what the Company stands for. In their sharing of this, a pattern showing what the organisation really values begins to emerge.

The golden rule here is to restrict the overall choice of values to four. How often have you seen long lists of 'values' that clearly have none, on account of the fact that the list is either too lengthy or too lazy?

Or, most commonly, both?

This section always provokes debate, as it should. If people don't feel passionate about their values, it's hard to see how they're going to feel passionate about the more mundane realities of their day-to-day working lives.

The values have to work for the Company in two ways. Internally, beyond technical ability, they're the measure by which people are hired, assessed and rewarded. Good leaders often talk about hiring 'for attitude, not aptitude.' It's a more succinct way of making this same point, as they are referring to the use of values as the arbiter of 'attitude.'

Externally, values are used to shape the organisation's personality. Again, they act as a filter through which all external communications should be processed before being allowed to run. This promotes consistency and, when done well, they have the additional benefit of being a vivid reminder for staff of what the Company stands for.

6. The 2-word summary

Having produced the Purpose statement based on motivations and competitive differences, and having given it texture and colour with values and Personality, the challenge for the team is to condense all of the thinking down to two words.

This is for the sake of memorability and portability.

It acts as a handbag for carrying all the relevant information, and makes it more readily useable for when the bullets are flying in the heat of the workplace.

'Reciprocated confidences' and 'Spirited Visioneering' are good examples. The mere recollection of the words brings with them a tide of other rich, meaty goodness, all of which can be brought to bear on the problem at hand, instantly.

But, perhaps above all, the real value of this is the sheer discipline of 'reductivist' thinking needed to decide – ultimately – what it is that lies at the very heart of the business.

It's incredibly hard to do – which is why most companies don't bother – but it's even more valuable than it is hard.

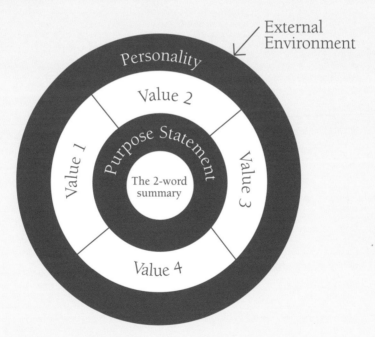

'No-one leaves the room until there's agreement.'

In conclusion

Of course, all of this dies a lingering death if it simply gets filed away in the 'good practice' folder and isn't enacted on. Articulating the Single Organising principle allows you and everyone else in the enterprise to wear it like a pair of spectacles, seeing life through the same, branded lenses.

And this is when the 'Great Humans' come into their own, to start championing the cause.

But where to start?

A good starting point is a 'misalignment measure.' Take an example (or two if you're ambitious), of an activity from each of the organisation's three circles, namely its Culture, its Product or Service and its Reputation.

For instance, consider the Induction programme (Culture), the Customer Services dept (Service) or the ingredients (Product, as relevant) and the website (Reputation).

Score each one out of seven against the agreed Values (maximum of four values, remember), and the 2-word summary itself. This simple exercise will act like a water-diviner for the Brand owner, as it will point out exactly where the discrepancies lie between the three areas.

Not only that, it'll help provide a detailed brief for what needs doing to make the organisation's graphic equalisers more... equal.

From then on it's a matter of making the Single Organising Principle meaningful and useful for each of the Company's three circles, led by the leaders and supported by the Champions.

But be warned. You will have just embarked on a life-long mission.

NOTES

The Single Organising Principle – the practice.

1 . Do you have a Single Organising Principle? Articulated in two words?

2. Does everyone in the Company know what they are and what they mean?

3. Is the Single Organising Principle being 'lived' in the Company's Culture, its Products and Services portfolio, and in its Reputation management?

Chapter 13
The Eskimos have got nothing on us

There's a debate about how many words the Inuit have for 'snow.' It ranges from four to 57. Either way, it suggests that snow is pretty important to them.

It might surprise you, then, to see how many words or phrases we have for the idea of the Single Organising Principle. If it's defined as 'the thing that drives us,' or 'the thing that governs us,' or 'what we're all about,' (there go three to start with…) then here's another batch:

the bottom line

the guts of it is

at the end of the day

hen all's said and done

at the heart of

when you really

fundamentally

get down to it

in a line

basically

in short

ultimately

quintessentially

definitively

central to my argument is

in essence

deep down

at the core

above all

he point is

let's get down to basics

first and foremost

brass tacks

elemental

bullseye

the bedrock

he be all and end all

period

end of

the foundation

full stop.

Rather than convoluted branding bollocks, I put it to you that the notion of the Single Organising Principle is one established from Natural Law and, really, as old as the hills.

And, some might argue, more useful.

And if it's at the epicentre (oops, there's another one…) of branding – which it is – then doesn't that make Brands and branding, and the Single Organising Principle in particular, as central to our lives as snow is to the Inuits?

In business terms, I believe that makes having a well-defined, well-understood and well-practised Single Organising Principle a lot more than a 'nice to have.'

NOTES

The Eskimos have got nothing on us.

1. Can you add to this list? (Come on, I'd be delighted to hear from you – robert.bean@northstarpartners.co.uk).

2. How central is The Single Organising Principle to you or your business?

3. If you had to produce a new 'Aunt Sally' version, what would it be?

I'm not a religious man, I'm more of a fundamentalist. But I do accept that religion has provided a sense of purpose for humanity that's deeper and longer-lasting than any political doctrine.

It gives people a belief system and an identity.

Like religion, a clear Brand pulls people in an organisation together, allowing them to worship at the same altar, irrespective of department or agenda.

Like religion, Brands can help you make decisions – things are either right or wrong. They fit or they don't.

And like religion, Brands give direction – providing everyone with their own vision of the cathedral whilst they're mixing their daily cement.

Finding and living your Brand's Single Organising Principle coherently, continuously and consistently is an exercise in self-definition that is an invaluable experience for everybody involved.

It's the fuel for how to win in your own way.

I cannot encourage you enough to take this journey for yourselves and your Brand. But I can guarantee that it will be every bit worth your while.

Acknowledgments

Much as this book has been about a personal trawl through what has mattered to me over many years of work – and still does – it's really only a collection of everything that other people have taught me.

The ones mentioned in the book speak for themselves. They're all big figures, making a difference in the world, and all winning in their own way.

But there are others. Lots of them. And they've been my secret weapons.

It all started with Jeannie. Not only did she prevent me from making a fool of myself when I was about to deliver a major speech, she also made me see the power of storytelling and so provided me with the basis of what would become a book.

But it was her ability to absorb, process, and re-constitute colossal amounts of information into digestible, well-ordered structure that was so breathtaking.

And she did it all without ever being anything other than elegant, composed and unruffled. I owe her a great deal.

Rosie has bestowed intellect, insights, intensity and an inordinate amount of interest in the book.

Beyond her insistence that I write it, (close observers might fairly have called it bullying), she also provided the original spark that led to the thinking around the Single Organising Principle. For her wisdom I am eternally grateful.

Anna, for being not just a rock, but a resourceful rock. Whenever I've got stuck she's always been there and, even when she's not there, just knowing she could be was help in itself.

She doesn't recognise problems; they're merely roundabouts to be got round.

Charlotte, one of those delightfully odd people who understands and articulates concepts with complete lucidity in conversation, but then thinks and expresses herself in pictures. She was organised enough to keep me on track, working out technical logistics, costs, timings and all the other practicalities of making it happen, whilst also being the creative and design source, translating my verbosity into visual language. It simply wouldn't have happened without her.

She has a peculiar and nearly perverse ambidextrous talent.

And she even looked like she was enjoying doing it.

Gerry, whose friendship I've exhausted, after he read, re-read and re-read again the various manuscripts. Only then to offer such sensible advice that it caused me to write, re-write and re-write again. Only then to cause him to read, re-read and re-read again, and on and on it went.

My thanks and apologies in equal measure. I pray he never writes one.

Eugene, for the kind use of the office, in which he suddenly interrupted a meeting one day with a stern "Now, Robert – Project Book." It was the moment I knew I couldn't wriggle out of it any more. It was also the spark that lit my enthusiasm for believing that I could actually do it. I'll be forever indebted for that.

Clare, who has been a great support and a great sport over the years; if only business could always be such fun.

Rufus, Trevor and Duncan, who have all contributed ideas and enthusiasm.

Hamish, who years ago said I should stop talking about it and just get on with it. I think it was an admonishment but I took it, inevitably, as personal support and encouragement. I never forgot it.

My dear Greek friend who's been there through thick and thin. He's the living embodiment of loyalty and generosity.

And my baby brother, whose help and guidance will never be forgotten.

But, above all, my thanks to Tori.

No-one has the right to be married to someone as supportive as her, so I know how blessed I am. She has unfailingly offered gentle help, sensible advice and fair criticism whenever I've sought it.

Best of all, she's managed to stay slim.

Life would have little Purpose if she wasn't around.

Image Credits

Special thanks to Steven Mallaby for many of the photographic images. (Many of them taken on Valentine's Day, which was not only a Saturday but also the day after his birthday…)
Magnus Spence and his artistic family for the illustrations
Jonny Rotten image courtesy of Richard E. Aaron / rockpix.com
The Body Shop Images reproduced by courtesy of The Body Shop International plc